Summary Information

	New Hires Can Enroll	Federal Benefits Open Season	How to Enroll	OPM's Program Website
FEHB	Within 60 days from new hire date	Annual – November 12 to December 10, 2012	Varies by agency; automated enrollment or via SF 2809	**www.opm.gov/insure/health**
FEDVIP	Within 60 days from new hire date	Annual – November 12 to December 10, 2012	Go to www.BENEFEDS.com or call 1-877-888-3337	**www.opm.gov/insure/dental** **www.opm.gov/insure/vision**
FSAFEDS	Within 60 days from new hire date	Annual – November 12 to December 10, 2012	Go to www.FSAFEDS.com or call 1-877-372-3337	**www.opm.gov/insure/flexible**
FEGLI	Within 60 days from new hire date for optional insurance; automatically enrolled in Basic insurance until you take action to cancel	No annual Open Season	Varies by agency; automated enrollment or via SF 2817 for new hires Others provide medical information on SF 2822	**www.opm.gov/insure/life**
FLTCIP	Apply (not necessarily enroll) within 60 days from new hire date with abbreviated underwriting	No annual Open Season	Go to www.LTCFEDS.com or call 1-800-582-3337	**www.opm.gov/insure/ltc**

Table of Contents

This page intentionally left blank

Introduction to Federal Benefits and This Guide

As a Federal employee, the benefits available to you represent a significant piece of your compensation package. They may provide important insurance coverage to protect you and your family and, in some cases, offer tax advantages that reduce the burden in paying for some health products and services, or dependent or elder care services.

The purpose of this Guide is to provide you basic information about the benefits offered to you as a Federal employee, and assist you in making informed choices about these benefits as you move through your career and prepare for retirement.

Benefits Programs included in this Guide

In addition to your Civil Service or Federal Employees Retirement System benefits and the Thrift Savings Plan, the Federal government offers five benefits programs to eligible employees and retirees. This Guide includes information on the five programs:

- Federal Employees Health Benefits Program
- Federal Employees Dental and Vision Insurance Program
- Federal Flexible Spending Account Program
- Federal Employees' Group Life Insurance Program
- Federal Long Term Care Insurance Program

If you are a new Federal employee or have recently become eligible for benefits, this Guide will walk you through the benefits offered and provide information on how and when to make your choices. If you are a current employee, this Guide will provide the most current information regarding the benefit programs, and will support you as you make decisions during the annual Federal Benefits Open Season, or experience life events that cause you to reconsider previous choices.

This Guide also contains some tips on what to consider as you make your decisions. For instance, did you know that the Federal Employees Health Benefits (FEHB) Program, the Federal Employees Dental and Vision Insurance Program (FEDVIP) and the Federal Flexible Spending Account Program (FSAFEDS) can potentially provide you with greater benefits without costing you much more? As a Federal employee, you can choose to pay the FEDVIP and FEHB premiums with pre-tax dollars and you can use pre-tax FSA dollars to pay for eligible expenses, including FEDVIP and FEHB copays and deductibles. Dental and vision care are also eligible FSA expenses, whether combined with FEDVIP coverage or not. Please take a moment to review the information in this Guide and decide upon the right choices for you.

Additional Information

You will find references throughout this Guide to websites or other locations to obtain more detailed information than is available here. We encourage you to access these sites to become a more educated decision-maker and consumer of Federal benefit programs.

Pre-Existing Condition Insurance Program (PCIP)

Do you know someone who needs health insurance but can't get it? The Pre-Existing Condition Insurance Plan (PCIP) may help.

An individual is eligible to buy coverage in PCIP if:

- He or she has a pre-existing medical condition or has been denied coverage because of the health condition;
- He or she has been without health coverage for at least the last six months. (If the individual currently has insurance coverage that does not cover the pre-existing condition or is enrolled in a state high risk pool then that person is not eligible for PCIP.);
- He or she is a citizen or national of the United States or resides in the U.S. legally.

The Federal government administers PCIP in the following states: Alabama, Arizona, District of Columbia, Delaware, Florida, Georgia, Hawaii, Idaho, Indiana, Kentucky, Louisiana, Massachusetts, Minnesota, Mississippi, North Dakota, Nebraska, Nevada, South Carolina, Tennessee, Texas, Vermont, Virginia, West Virginia, and Wyoming. To find out about eligibility, visit www.pcip.gov and/or www.healthcare.gov or call 1-866-717-5826 (TTY: 1-866-561-1604).

New or Newly Eligible Employees

As a new or newly eligible employee, you may have the opportunity to enroll in the benefit programs noted below. Use this chart to assist you with the decision-making process of selecting and enrolling in the benefit programs below that meet your needs. The chart gives you things to consider as you make your decisions.

FEHB	1. See page 10 for general information on FEHB (including eligibility) and for guidance on choosing a plan; 2. If you decide to enroll, examine the 2013 brochure of each plan you consider to ensure the benefits and premiums meet your needs and the plan is available in your area; 3. Contact the human resources office of your agency for information on how to enroll.
FEDVIP	1. See page 14 for general information on FEDVIP (including eligibility) and guidance on choosing a FEDVIP dental plan and/or vision plan; 2. If you decide to enroll, examine the 2013 brochure of each plan you consider to ensure the benefits and premiums meet your needs and the plan is available in your area; 3. See page 16 for information on how to enroll.
FSAFEDS	1. See page 18 for general information on FSAFEDS (including eligibility) and for guidance on making a decision whether to participate; 2. See page 21 for information on how to enroll.
FEGLI	1. See page 22 for general information on FEGLI (including eligibility) and for guidance on making a decision whether to select optional insurance (Basic FEGLI is automatic); 2. See page 23 for information on how to enroll.
FLTCIP	1. See page 24 for general information on FLTCIP (including eligibility) and for guidance on making a decision whether to apply; 2. See page 25 for information on how to apply for coverage.

Current Employees

During Open Season, you have the opportunity to enroll or make changes in the Federal Employees Health Benefits (FEHB) Program, the Federal Employees Dental and Vision Insurance Program (FEDVIP) and the Federal Flexible Spending Account Program (FSAFEDS). You can use this chart to assist you with the decision-making process of selecting plans and enrolling in these benefit programs.

	If Currently Enrolled in the Program	**If Not Enrolled in the Program**
FEHB	1. Check your plan's 2013 premiums and satisfaction survey results in Appendix E; 2. Examine your plan's 2013 brochure for benefit and enrollment/service area changes; 3. Check Appendix E for any new plans and plan options available to you; 4. If satisfied with your plan's rates, survey results and benefits for 2013, **do nothing** – your enrollment will continue automatically; 5. If **not** satisfied with your current plan for 2013, see Appendix B for guidance on choosing another plan. 6. See page 7 for information on FEHB and retirement.	1. See page 10 for general information on FEHB (including eligibility) and Appendix B for guidance on choosing a plan; 2. If you decide to enroll, examine the 2013 brochure of each plan you consider to ensure the benefits and premiums meet your needs and the plan is available in your area; 3. Contact the human resources office of your agency for information on how to enroll.
FEDVIP	1. Check your plan's 2013 premiums in Appendix K and examine your plan's 2013 brochure for benefit and enrollment/service area changes; 2. If also enrolled in FEHB, check your 2013 FEHB brochure for any changes in dental and/or vision benefits; 3. If satisfied with your plan's rates and benefits for 2013, **do nothing** – your enrollment will continue automatically; 4. If **not** satisfied with your current plan for 2013, see page 16 for guidance on choosing another plan and for information on how to change your enrollment; 5. If you no longer want FEDVIP, you must cancel during Open Season by contacting BENEFEDS. After Open Season you cannot cancel; see Appendix H for details. 6. See page 8 for information on FEDVIP and retirement.	1. See page 14 for general information on FEDVIP (including eligibility) and for guidance on choosing a FEDVIP plan; 2. If you decide to enroll, examine the 2013 brochure of the plans in which you are interested to ensure the benefits and premiums meet your needs and the plan is available in your area; 3. If enrolled in FEHB, check your 2013 FEHB brochure for any changes in dental and/or vision benefits. 4. See page 16 for information on how to enroll.
FSAFEDS	1. If you want to participate in 2013, **you must make a new election**. Keep in mind your election and enrollment do **not** carry over from year to year; see page for information on how to enroll; 2. Check your 2013 FEHB and 2013 FEDVIP plan brochures to see how any benefit changes may affect your out-of-pocket health care expenses; 3. See page 18 for any updated information about the Program.	1. See page 18 for general information on FSAFEDS (including eligibility) and for guidance on making a decision whether to participate; 2. See page 21 for information on how to enroll.

Federal Benefits Facts

FEHB

- When you retire, you are eligible to continue health benefits coverage if you meet all of the following requirements:
  - you are entitled to retire on an immediate annuity under a retirement system for civilian employees (including the Federal Employees Retirement System (FERS) Minimum Retirement Age (MRA) + 10 retirement); and
  - you have been continuously enrolled (or covered as a family member) in any FEHB plan(s) for the 5 years of service immediately before your retirement date, or for the full period(s) of service since your first opportunity to enroll (if less than 5 years).

- The 5 year requirement period can include the following:
  - the time you are covered as a family member under another person's FEHB enrollment; or
  - the time you are covered under the Uniformed Services Health Benefits Program (also known as TRICARE) as long as you were covered under an FEHB enrollment at the time of your retirement.

- As an annuitant, you are entitled to the same benefits and Government contributions as Federal employees enrolled in the same plan.

- The event of retirement is not a qualifying life event (QLE); however, there are other opportunities to change FEHB enrollment including during Open Season or when you experience a QLE.

- If you retire with a Self Only enrollment and later want to cover eligible family members, you can change to a Self and Family enrollment during the annual Open Season or when you experience certain QLEs.

- If you are not enrolled in FEHB (or covered as a family member) at the time of your retirement, you cannot enroll when you retire.

- If you are enrolled in a High Deductible Health Plan (HDHP) with a Health Savings Account (HSA) at the time of your retirement, you can still contribute to your HSA provided you have no other insurance coverage other than those specifically allowed, and are not claimed as a dependent on someone else's tax return. Some examples of other coverage that would cause ineligibility are: Medicare, TRICARE, other non-high deductible health insurance, or having received VA benefits within the previous three months. If you don't qualify for an HSA, your plan will enroll you in a Health Reimbursement Arrangement (HRA).

- If you cancel your FEHB enrollment as an annuitant, you will never be able to re-enroll in FEHB **unless** you had suspended your FEHB enrollment because you are now covered by a Medicare Advantage plan, TRICARE or CHAMPVA, Medicaid or similar State-sponsored program of medical assistance, or Peace Corps Volunteer coverage.

- If you want your surviving family members to continue your health benefits enrollment after your death, you must be enrolled for Self and Family at the time of your death, and at least one family member must be entitled to an annuity as your survivor.

- Consider whether you need to sign up for Medicare when you become eligible.

Federal Benefits Facts *continued*

FEDVIP

- There is no 5 year requirement for continuing FEDVIP coverage into retirement.

- Your coverage will continue as a retiree. Retirees may also enroll during the annual Federal Benefits Open Season or when you experience a qualifying life event (QLE). Keep in mind that **retirement is not a QLE**.

- In most cases, changing from payroll deduction to annuity deduction is automatic, but may take several months to occur. It is advised that you contact BENEFEDS at 1-877-888-3337 prior to retirement in order to eliminate any suspension in coverage.

- BENEFEDS cannot deduct premiums from your annuity while you are receiving "special" or "interim" pay. Once your annuity is finalized, premium deductions will begin. If you miss one or more premium payments before your annuity is final, BENEFEDS will make double deductions until any balance due is paid. They will notify you before deducting this additional premium amount. Once there is no past due balance, the amount of premium deducted will return to the regular monthly premium.

FSAFEDS

- When you retire, you will no longer be able to participate in FSAFEDS. Your FSA will terminate as of the date of your retirement, and you will not be eligible to enroll as an annuitant. When you make your annual election for the year that you plan to retire, keep in mind that any remaining funds for which you have not incurred eligible expenses while employed will be forfeited.

- You can still submit claims for eligible medical expenses incurred prior to the date of your retirement.

- You can continue to use the remaining balance in your Dependent Care Flexible Spending Account (DCFSA) to pay for eligible dependent care expenses until the end of the Benefit Period or until your account balance is used up, whichever comes first.

Federal Benefits Facts *continued*

FEGLI

- When you retire, you are eligible to continue your FEGLI life insurance coverage(s) if you retire on an immediate annuity and had the coverage for:
  - the five years of service immediately before the starting date of your annuity or, for annuitants retiring under FERS who postpone receiving their annuity, the five years immediately before their separation date for annuity purposes, or
  - all period(s) of service during which that coverage was available to you if it is less than five years, and
  - you (or your assignees) do not convert the coverage to a private policy.
- If you are eligible, you will choose via Standard Form (SF) 2818 how you wish your coverage(s) to continue during your retirement.
- If you are not enrolled in FEGLI at the time of your retirement, you cannot enroll when you retire.
- You cannot newly elect or increase existing coverage after you retire. You may only reduce or cancel coverage.
- Your premiums are subject to change in the future. Your premium could change based on your age and the experience of the Program. You will be notified if there is any change in your deductions from your annuity.

FLTCIP

- Your coverage continues into retirement provided you continue to pay premiums.
- If you pay premiums via payroll deduction, then shortly before you retire, you should notify Long Term Care Partners (LTCP) at 1-800-582-3337 to make other arrangements for premium payment.
- You may elect annuity deduction if you desire. LTCP cannot deduct your premium from "special" or "interim" pay. LTCP will send you a direct bill during this time. Premium deduction will begin from your annuity once it is finalized.

Federal Employees Health Benefits (FEHB) Program

What does this Program offer?

The FEHB Program offers a wide variety of plans and coverage to help you meet your health care needs. It is group coverage available to employees, retirees and their eligible family members. If you continuously maintain your FEHB enrollment, or are covered by another FEHB enrollment as a family member, or a combination of both, for the five years of service immediately preceding your retirement or the full period(s) of service since your first opportunity to enroll if less than five years, and you retire on an immediate annuity, you can continue to participate in the FEHB Program after retirement. The benefits you receive as a retiree are the same coverage Federal employees receive and at the same cost. If you leave government employment before retiring, the Program offers temporary continuation of coverage (TCC) and an opportunity to convert your enrollment to non-group (private) coverage.

If you are currently enrolled in the FEHB Program and do not want to change plans or enrollment type during Open Season, you do not need to do anything. Your enrollment will continue automatically.

Appendix E includes a comparison chart of all the plans in the FEHB Program with information comparing basic benefits and costs.

Key FEHB facts

- The FEHB Program is part of the annual Federal Benefits Open Season.

- FEHB coverage continues each year. You do not need to re-enroll each year. If you are happy with your current coverage, do nothing. Please note that your premiums and benefits may change.

- You can choose from Consumer-Driven and High Deductible plans that offer catastrophic risk protection with higher deductibles, health savings/reimbursement accounts and lower premiums, or Health Maintenance Organizations or Fee-for-Service plans with comprehensive coverage and higher premiums.

- There are no waiting periods and no pre-existing condition limitations, even if you change plans.

- If you are an active Federal employee, you can use your Health Care Flexible Spending Account or Limited Expense Health Care Flexible Spending Account with your FEHB plan.

- If you participate in premium conversion, enrollment changes can only be made during Open Season or if you experience a qualifying life event. Premium conversion allows Federal employees to use pre-tax dollars to pay their FEHB premiums. If you do not participate in premium conversion, you may change to Self Only or cancel at any time.

- All nationwide FEHB plans offer international coverage.

- There are separate and/or different provider networks for each plan.

- Utilizing an in-network provider will reduce your out-of-pocket costs.

What enrollment types are available?

- Self Only, which covers only the enrolled employee; or
- Self and Family, which covers the enrolled employee and all eligible family members.

Which family members are eligible?

Family Members covered under your Self and Family enrollment are:

- Your spouse (including a valid common law marriage); and

- Children under age 26, including recognized natural children, legally adopted children, and stepchildren.

Foster children are included if they meet certain requirements. A child age 26 or over who is incapable of self-support because of a mental or physical disability that existed before age 26 is also an eligible family member.

Contact your employing office for additional information. In determining whether the child is a covered family member, your employing office will look at the child's relationship to you as an enrollee.

How much does it cost?

The premiums for your enrollment are shared by you and your Federal agency or retirement system. The government pays the lesser of: 72% of the average total premium of all plans weighted by the number of enrollees in each, or 75% of the premium for the specific plan you choose. If you are an employee, you automatically pay your share of the premium through a payroll deduction using pre-tax dollars, unless you elect not to participate in Premium Conversion. The charts in Appendix E provide cost information for all plans in the FEHB Program.

Am I eligible to enroll?

Most employees are eligible; those who are not eligible usually have limited appointments of short duration, or work sporadically only during certain seasons or when needed by their Federal agency. If you have an appointment other than a career or career conditional appointment and your agency has not provided you information about enrollment, you should contact your human resources office for information.

When you retire, you are eligible to continue health benefits coverage if you retire on an immediate annuity under a retirement system for civilian employees (including FERS MRA + 10 retirement) and you have been continuously enrolled (or covered as a family member) in any FEHB plan(s) for the 5 years of service immediately before your retirement date, or for the full period(s) of service since your first opportunity to enroll (if less than 5 years).

If you suspend your FEHB coverage as a retiree because you are covered by TRICARE or CHAMPVA, a Medicare Advantage Plan, Medicaid, or Peace Corps volunteer coverage, you may reenroll under certain conditions. (You should contact your retirement system for information on your eligibility.) **If you are not enrolled in or covered as a family member under FEHB when you retire, you will not be able to enroll after retirement.**

Federal Employees Health Benefits (FEHB) Program

When can I enroll or change my enrollment?

If you are a new employee who is eligible for FEHB or an employee who has become newly eligible to enroll, you may enroll within 60 days of becoming eligible. You may also enroll during the annual Open Season held from the Monday of the second full work week in November through the Monday of the second full work week in December. Furthermore, you may enroll, change your enrollment type, or change plans outside of Open Season if you experience a qualifying life event such as a change in family or other insurance coverage status. Appendix C contains more specific information about qualifying life events that permit employees to enroll or change enrollment in the FEHB Program.

For new or newly eligible employees who elect to enroll, coverage will be effective on the first day of the first pay period that begins after your agency receives your enrollment. An Open Season enrollment or change is effective on the first day of the first full pay period that begins in January.

Note: Certain pay status requirements may also apply. Your Human Resources Office can advise you of your specific effective date.

How do I enroll or change my enrollment?

You may be able to enroll or change your enrollment using the Health Benefits Election Form (SF 2809) or through an agency self-service system such as Employee Express, MyPay, Employee Personal Page, or EBIS. Contact the human resources office of your employing agency for details.

How do I get more information about this Program?

Visit the FEHB Program online at www.opm.gov/insure/health for information including:
- How to compare and choose among health plans
- Health plan websites and plan brochures
- How to file a disputed claim request
- Getting quality healthcare
- Medicare and FEHB

Did You Know... Health Information Technology can improve your health!

What is Health Information Technology? Health Information Technology (HIT) allows doctors and hospitals to manage medical information and to securely exchange information among patients and providers. In a variety of ways, HIT has a demonstrated benefit in improving health care quality, preventing medical errors, reducing costs, and decreasing paperwork.

What are examples of HIT at work?

- You can go online to review your medical, pharmacy, and laboratory claims information;

- If you complete a Health Risk Assessment (HRA), your health plan can identify you as a candidate for case management or disease management and offer suggestions on healthy lifestyle strategies and how to reduce or eliminate health risks. Health plans can provide you with tips and educational material about good health habits, information about routine care that is age and gender appropriate.

- Physicians can have the very best clinical guidelines at their fingertips for managing and treating diseases;

- While with a patient, a physician can enter a prescription on a computer where potential allergies and adverse reactions are shown immediately;

- Computer alerts are sent to physicians to remind them of a patient's preventive care needs and to track referrals and test results.

One feature of HIT is the **Personal Health Record (PHR)**. The electronic version of your medical records allows you to maintain and manage health information for yourself and your family in a private and secure electronic environment. Some health plans include your medical claims data in your PHR, which gives a more complete picture of your health status and history.

You can also find a PHR on OPM's website at www.opm.gov/insure/health/phr/tools.asp. This PHR is a fillable and downloadable form that you complete yourself and save on your home computer. We encourage you to take a look at this PHR option and, if you determine it will fulfill your record-keeping needs, take advantage of this opportunity.

Price/cost transparency is another element of health information technology. For example, many health plans allow you to use online tools that will show what the plan will pay on average for a specific procedure or for a specific prescription drug. You can also review healthcare quality indicators for physician and hospital services.

The health plans listed on our HIT website at www.opm.gov/insure/health/reference/hittransparency.asp have taken steps to help you become a better consumer of health care and have met OPM's HIT, quality and price/cost transparency standards.

No one is more responsible for your health care than you – HIT tools can help.

What does this Program offer?

The Federal Employees Dental and Vision Insurance Program provides comprehensive dental and vision insurance at competitive group rates. There are seven dental plans and three vision plans from which to choose. FEDVIP features nationwide, international, and regional plans.

A dental or vision insurance plan is much like a health insurance plan; you may be required to meet a deductible and provide a copay or coinsurance payments for your dental or vision services. With any plan choice, you should look at all the information and find a plan that will best fit your needs. You should also review your FEHB plan brochure to determine what dental and/or vision coverage the FEHB plan provides.

If you are currently enrolled in FEDVIP and you take no action during Open Season, your current coverage will continue in 2013, provided you remain eligible for the program. Enrollment continues year to year, automatically. **Please Note:** your premiums and benefits may change for 2013.

Key FEDVIP facts

- FEDVIP is part of the annual Federal Benefits Open Season.
- FEDVIP is separate and different from the FEHB Program.
- The health care law does not change the age or unmarried requirement for dependents in FEDVIP.
- FEDVIP coverage continues each year. You do not need to re-enroll each year. If you do not want to change plans or enrollment type, do nothing.
- You can only cancel FEDVIP coverage during Open Season, upon deployment to active military duty or upon transfer to another agency where you enroll in their dental and/or vision plan and the agency pays at least 50% of the premium. You cannot cancel just because you retire or because you can no longer afford the premiums.
- If you are enrolled in an FEHB plan, it is a requirement under the FEDVIP law that your FEHB plan function as the first payer. The FEDVIP plan is always the secondary payer to the FEHB plan.
- You can use your Flexible Spending Account (FSAFEDS) with FEDVIP. You can submit your FEDVIP copayments and deductibles as eligible expenses against your FSA account.
- All nationwide FEDVIP plans provide international coverage.
- There are separate and/or different provider networks for each plan.
- Utilizing an in-network provider will reduce your out-of-pocket costs.
- There are no pre-existing condition limitations for enrollment.
- There is no opportunity to convert to a private plan when your FEDVIP coverage ends. There is no 31-day extension of coverage, Temporary Continuation of Coverage (TCC), Spouse Equity coverage, or right to convert to an individual policy (conversion policy).

What enrollment types are available?

- Self Only, which covers only the enrolled employee or retiree;
- Self Plus One, which covers the enrolled employee or retiree plus one eligible family member specified by the enrollee; and
- Self and Family, which covers the enrolled employee or retiree and all eligible family members.

Appendix I lists the available dental and vision insurance plans along with basic benefit information.

Which family members are eligible?

Eligible family members include your spouse and unmarried dependent children under age 22. This includes legally adopted children and recognized natural children who meet certain dependency requirements. This also includes stepchildren and foster children who live with you in a regular parent-child relationship. Under certain circumstances, you may also continue coverage for a disabled child 22 years of age or older who is incapable of self-support. In order to determine whether your dependent child age 22 or over is incapable of self-support, you may be asked to provide a medical certificate that describes a disability with onset prior to age 22; or acceptable documentation that the medical condition is not compatible with employment, that there is a medical reason to restrict your child from working, or that he/she may suffer injury or harm by working.

FEDVIP rules and FEHB rules for family member eligibility are **NOT** the same.

Note: Changes in dependent eligibility under healthcare reform (Affordable Care Act) do not affect eligibility for children under FEDVIP.

How much does it cost?

You pay the entire premium. There is no government contribution to the premium. If you are an active employee, your premiums are taken from your salary on a pre-tax basis if your salary is sufficient to make the premium withholding. When you retire, premiums are withheld from your monthly annuity check on a post-tax basis if your annuity is sufficient.

Premiums for the nationwide dental plans and one regional dental plan are based on where you live. This is called your rating region. Your home ZIP code is used to find your rating region. Rating regions vary by carrier. The vision plans do not have rating regions. Enrolling in a FEDVIP plan will not reduce your FEHB premium.

See Appendices J and K to find 1) the rating region assigned to the area where you live by the different dental plans and 2) the related premium you will pay. You may also go to our website at www.opm.gov/insure/dental and www.opm.gov/insure/vision for premium and rating region information.

Am I eligible to enroll?

In general, Federal employees eligible for FEHB coverage (whether or not actually enrolled) and retirees (regardless of FEHB status) are eligible to enroll in a dental and/or vision plan. Former spouses and deferred annuitants are NOT eligible to enroll. Anyone receiving an insurable interest annuity who is not also an eligible family member is NOT eligible to enroll.

When can I enroll or change my enrollment?

If you are a new employee eligible for FEDVIP, or an employee who has become newly eligible to enroll, you may enroll within 60 days of first becoming eligible. This is a one-time opportunity outside of Open Season to enroll. There is a separate 60-day enrollment period for dental and vision. For example: you may enroll in a dental plan on day 30 and a vision plan on day 59. Once you enroll, your 60-day opportunity for that type of plan ends.

An eligible employee or retiree may also enroll during the annual Federal Benefits Open Season, which runs from the Monday of the second full work week in November through the Monday of the second full work week in December. An eligible employee or retiree may enroll, cancel, or change enrollment type or options during Open Season. They may enroll or make changes outside of Open Season if they experience a qualifying life event (QLE) such as a change in family or other insurance coverage status. Please see Appendix H for more information about QLEs that permit employees and retirees to enroll or make changes in FEDVIP.

If you enroll during Open Season, premiums are deducted beginning the first full pay period on or after January 1. For new or newly eligible employees who elect to enroll, coverage is effective the first day of the pay period following the one in which BENEFEDS receives your enrollment. An Open Season enrollment or change is effective January 1.

How do I enroll or change my enrollment?

You may enroll on the Internet at www.BENEFEDS.com. BENEFEDS is a secure enrollment website sponsored by OPM. For those without access to a computer, please call 1-877-888-FEDS (1-877-888-3337) (TTY number, 1-877-889-5680).

You cannot enroll in a FEDVIP plan using the Health Benefits Election Form (SF 2809) or through an agency self-service system, such as Employee Express, MyPay or Employee Personal Page. However, those sites may provide a link to BENEFEDS.

What should I consider in making my decision to participate in this Program?

There are questions you should ask yourself when deciding to enroll in FEDVIP or selecting a FEDVIP plan. By considering these questions thoroughly, you will be able to determine if FEDVIP is a good option for you.

1. Does my FEHB plan provide dental or vision coverage?

2. Does the FEDVIP plan coordinate benefits with the FEHB plan and how is the coordination of benefits calculated?

3. How affordable is the plan?
   - How much will it cost me on a bi-weekly or monthly basis? Can I afford that for the entire year?
   - Must I pay a deductible?
   - If I use a FEDVIP provider outside of the network, how much will I pay to get care?
   - How frequently can I visit the dentist and how much do I have to pay at each visit?
   - Will the plan provide benefits if I am also covered by another dental or vision plan?

4. Do I have access to any provider?
   - Does the plan give me the freedom to choose my own dentist or am I restricted to a panel of dentists selected by the plan?
   - Are there enough of the kinds of dentists I want to see?
   - Where will I go for care? Are these places near where I work or live?
   - Do I need to get permission before I see a dental specialist?
   - Will the plan allow referrals to specialists? Will my dentist and I be able to choose the specialist?

5. Does the plan provide coverage for specialty services?
   - Are dentures, orthodontics, implants or replacement of missing teeth covered?
   - What are the plan's limitations or exclusions?
   - Are there annual limits on the types of services included?

How do I find my premium rate?

If you live outside the United States:
Go to Appendix K for your dental and vision premium rates.

If you live inside the United States:
Go to Appendix K for your vision premium rate. To find your bi-weekly or monthly dental premium, you must first find your rating area on the chart in Appendix J. Some plans may have changed their rating regions for the upcoming plan year.

Please Note: If you are currently enrolled and have moved or your postal service has assigned you a new ZIP code, your rating region may have changed.

1. To find your dental rating area:
   a. Go to the chart in Appendix J.
   b. Find your state and your corresponding Zip code (1st 3 digits).
   c. Look under the plan name and you will find your rating area.

2. To find your bi-weekly or monthly dental premium, match your rating area with your desired FEDVIP plan on the chart in Appendix K.

Making an informed choice

- Before selecting a plan that best suits your needs, ask your carrier or access the OPM website for a copy of the plan brochure.
- If you have questions about coverage, exclusions, limitations or payment of benefits, ask the plan before making your plan selection.
- Find out which plan your provider participates in and why. Keep in mind that if your provider leaves the plan, this is not a qualifying life event allowing a change or cancellation.

How do I get more information about this Program?

Visit FEDVIP online at www.opm.gov/insure/dental and www.opm.gov/insure/vision for information including:
- How to enroll
- FEDVIP plan websites, brochures, and provider searches
- Dental premium rates
- Vision premium rates

Federal Flexible Spending Account Program (FSAFEDS)

What does this Program offer?

A way to SAVE MONEY. The Federal Flexible Spending Account Program, known as FSAFEDS, is a benefit that can save you money. It offers accounts where you contribute money from your salary BEFORE taxes are withheld, incur eligible expenses, and get reimbursed. It's a way to save money on dependent care and health care services and items for you and your family. It's a way to pay less tax and save money!

The money contributed to your FSAFEDS account is set aside before taxes are deducted, so in most cases you save about 30% on your Federal taxes. The average tax savings for a person earning $50,000 who contributes $2,000 into an FSA account is approximately $600. That means you get $2000 worth of FSA eligible purchasing power PLUS pay about $600 LESS in Federal taxes.

Key FSAFEDS facts

- FSAFEDS is part of the annual Federal Benefits Open Season.
- Retirees cannot enroll in FSAFEDS.
- Employees MUST re-enroll each year – coverage does not automatically carry over to the next benefit period.
- If you enroll during Open Season you will have 14-1/2 months to spend your annual election.
- Enrollees must incur eligible expenses for their current benefit period by March 15th of the following year.
- Enrollees must file claims for their current benefit period by April 30th of the following year.
- Enrollees can use FSAFEDS accounts for copayments and deductibles from their FEHB and/or FEDVIP enrollments.
- Plan your contribution carefully and conservatively – you will lose any money in your account(s) for which you do not incur eligible expenses and timely file claims.
- Eligible health care expenses of an employee's child are covered through the end of the year in which the child turns 26.

Recent changes to FSAFEDS

- Coverage for Over-the-Counter Medicines or Drugs - Over-the-counter (OTC) products that are medicines or drugs are not eligible for reimbursement from your Health Care FSA – unless – you have a prescription for that item written by your physician. The only exception is insulin – you will not need a prescription. Other currently eligible OTC items that are not medicines or drugs will not require a prescription.
- Expanded Coverage for Your Child's Eligible Health Care Expenses - An employee enrolled in FSAFEDS may request reimbursement for eligible health care expenses incurred by a natural child, stepchild, adopted child, eligible foster child, or a child who is placed with the employee for legal adoption. The child does not need to reside with the employee or qualify as the employee's tax dependent.
- The Health Care and Limited Expense Health Care FSA maximum election is changed from $5,000 to $2,500.

What enrollment types are available?

There are three types of FSAs. Each type has a minimum annual election of $250 and the Dependent Care FSA has a maximum of $5,000. The Health Care FSA and Limited Expense FSA have a maximum annual election of $2,500.

- **Dependent Care FSA (DCFSA)** – Used for eligible dependent care (non-medical) expenses that allow you and your spouse (if married) to work, look for work (as long as you have earned income at some point during the year), or attend school full-time. Eligible expenses include child care, before and after school care, late pick-up fees, and adult daycare. Dependents covered under a DCFSA include your children before their 13th birthday, and may also include any person you claim as a dependent on your Federal Income Tax return who is mentally or physically incapable of self care.

- **Health Care FSA (HCFSA)** – Used for eligible health care expenses for you, your spouse, your tax dependents, and your adult children through the end of the calendar year in which they turn age 26 that are not covered or reimbursed by FEHB, FEDVIP or other insurance. Common expenses that are reimbursable by an HCFSA include:

  - Chiropractic services
  - Coinsurance, copays and deductibles (but not insurance premiums)
  - Contact lenses, solutions, and cleaners and cases
  - Dental care and procedures
  - Eye surgery
  - Eyeglasses and prescription sunglasses
  - Hearing aids and batteries
  - Infertility treatments

  An HCFSA is not health insurance and does not replace your insurance plan. It is a separate program that reimburses you for eligible out-of-pocket health care expenses.

- **Limited Expense Health Care FSA (LEX HCFSA)** – Designed for employees enrolled in or covered by a High Deductible Health Plan with a Health Savings Account. Eligible expenses are **limited** to dental and vision care expenses for you, your spouse, your tax dependents and your adult children through the end of the calendar year in which they turn age 26 that are not covered or reimbursed by FEHB, FEDVIP or other insurance. By opening a Limited Expense Health Care FSA you can save money on taxes by using your LEX HCFSA dollars for dental and vision care while preserving your Health Savings Account funds for other purposes.

  Eligible expenses include your out-of-pocket costs for services and products related to:
  – Dental care (e.g., cleanings, fillings, crowns, orthodontics, etc.)
  – Vision care (e.g., contact lenses, eyeglasses, refractions, vision correction procedures, etc.)

Am I eligible to enroll?

Most Federal employees in the Executive branch and many in non-Executive branch agencies are eligible. For specifics on eligibility, visit www.FSAFEDS.com or call an

FSAFEDS Benefits Counselor toll-free at 1-877-FSAFEDS (1-877-372-3337) TTY: 1-800-952-0450, Monday through Friday, 9 a.m. until 9 p.m., Eastern Time. Retirees cannot enroll.

Which family members are eligible?

Enrollees in FSAFEDS may request reimbursement for eligible health care expenses incurred by a spouse, tax dependent, natural child, stepchild, adopted child, eligible foster child, or a child who is placed with the enrollee for legal adoption.

When can I enroll or change my enrollment?

If you are a new or newly eligible employee or experience a qualifying life event (QLE), such as a change in family status, you have 60 days from your hire date (QLE date) to enroll in a HCFSA or LEX HCFSA and/or DCFSA, but you must enroll before October 1. If you are hired or become eligible or experience a QLE on or after October 1, you must wait and enroll during the Federal Benefits Open Season held each fall, which runs from the Monday of the second full work week in November to the Monday of the second full work week in December. You can find more information about qualifying life events at www.FSAFEDS.com.

Enrollment does not carry over from year to year – you must make an election every year to participate!

An election made during Open Season is effective on January 1 of the benefit year. If you are a newly hired or newly eligible employee enrolling outside of Open Season, your effective date is the day after your election is accepted by FSAFEDS.

Qualifying Life Events (QLEs) that May Permit a Change in Your Flexible Spending Account Participation

The following QLEs may allow you to enroll, cancel, increase, or even decrease your election amount:

- A change in your legal marital status (i.e., marriage, legal separation, divorce, or death of your spouse)
- The birth or adoption of your child, or placement for adoption
- The death of a dependent
- Other changes in the number of your tax dependents (e.g., parents now reside with you because they are incapable of self-care)
- A change in employment status (for you, your spouse or your dependent) that affects eligibility for health insurance benefits
- Leave Without Pay (LWOP) due to military deployment
- A change in your dependent's eligibility (e.g., your child reaches age 13 when he/she is no longer eligible for coverage under a Dependent Care Flexible Spending Account)
- A change in cost or coverage for daycare or elder care (e.g., a significant cost increase charged by your current daycare provider, or a change in your provider – for Dependent Care Flexible Spending Account only)

How do I enroll?

You enroll at www.FSAFEDS.com or by calling 1-877-372-3337.

What should I consider in making my decision to participate in this Program?

- Do I want to participate this year? You must make a new election every year. Enrollment does not carry over from year to year.
- What do my annual medical/dependent care out-of-pocket expenses run each year?
- Will my health, dental or vision insurance coverage be different this year? Am I changing plans or adding other coverage? Are my copayments changing?
- Will I still have the same number of dependents?
- **Plan your contribution carefully and conservatively – you will lose any money in your account(s) for which you do not incur eligible expenses and timely file claims.**

How do I get more information about this Program?

Call 1-877-372-3337, TTY 1-800-952-0450, or visit www.FSAFEDS.com.

Federal Employees' Group Life Insurance (FEGLI) Program

What does this Program offer?

The FEGLI Program offers group term life insurance.

Key FEGLI facts

- The FEGLI Program is **not** part of the annual Federal Benefits Open Season.
- Employees in eligible positions are automatically covered under Basic life insurance, unless they choose to waive that coverage.
- Employees must have Basic insurance in order to have or elect Optional insurance.
- Employees must take action, within strict time limits, to elect Optional insurance. Coverage is not automatic.
- The Government pays one-third of the cost of Basic insurance. Enrollees pay 100% of the cost of Optional insurance.
- FEGLI does not have any cash or paid-up value. You cannot get a loan by borrowing from this insurance.
- Retirees may be able to continue their FEGLI coverage into retirement, but they cannot newly elect FEGLI coverage as a retiree.
- Living benefits are life insurance benefits paid to you while you are still living, rather than paid to a beneficiary or survivor when you die. You are eligible to elect a living benefit if you are an employee, retiree, or compensationer covered under the FEGLI Program who has been diagnosed as terminally ill with a life expectancy of nine months or less, and you have not assigned your insurance.

What coverage is available?

Basic insurance – your annual salary, rounded up to the next even $1,000, plus $2,000. Basic insurance includes accidental death and dismemberment coverage for employees (not for retirees).

Optional insurance
- **Option A - Standard** – $10,000 of insurance. Option A includes accidental death and dismemberment coverage for employees (not for retirees).
- **Option B - Additional** – 1, 2, 3, 4 or 5 times your annual rate of basic pay after rounding it up to the next even $1,000.
- **Option C - Family** – coverage for your spouse and all of your eligible dependent children. You can elect 1, 2, 3, 4 or 5 multiples. Each multiple is equal to $5,000 for your spouse and $2,500 for each eligible child.

How much does it cost?

You pay two-thirds of the premium for Basic life insurance and the Government pays one-third. Your cost for Basic life insurance is $0.15 biweekly, per $1,000 of coverage. Your age does not affect the cost of Basic insurance.

You pay 100% of the premium for Optional insurance. The cost depends on your age, based on 5-year age groups.

Am I eligible to enroll?

Most Federal employees are eligible to enroll in FEGLI unless they are excluded by law or regulation. Federal retirees are eligible to carry their FEGLI into retirement if they meet the following requirements: eligible to retire on an immediate annuity (including FERS MRA+10 retirement), have not converted the coverage to a private plan, and have been insured under FEGLI for the five years immediately preceding retirement or for all periods of service during which FEGLI was available to them if they have been covered for less than five years. **There is no waiver of this five-year rule.**

Which family members are eligible?

Eligible FEGLI family members include a spouse and eligible dependent children. Eligible dependent children must be unmarried and under age 22, or if age 22 or over, incapable of self-support because of a mental or physical disability that existed before the child reached age 22. Eligible dependent children include your natural children, adopted children, stepchildren (if they live with you in a regular parent-child relationship), and foster children (if they live with you in a regular parent-child relationship). Stillborn children are not covered.

When can I enroll or change my enrollment?

The FEGLI Program is **not** part of the annual Federal Benefits Open Season.

If you are a new employee who is eligible for FEGLI, or an employee who has become newly eligible to enroll, you will be automatically enrolled in Basic. If you do not want Basic, you must file a waiver with your agency.

As a new or newly eligible employee, you may enroll in Optional insurance within 60 days of becoming eligible. If you take no action, you will have Basic and will not have any Optional insurance.

If you are not a new employee or newly eligible, you may enroll in Basic life insurance and, if you wish, Option A and/or Option B coverage by providing satisfactory medical information at your own expense using the Request for Life Insurance (Standard Form 2822). You cannot enroll in Option C this way.

You may elect Basic, Option A, Option B and Option C within 60 days of a FEGLI qualifying life event. In addition, you may increase the number of multiples of Option B and/or Option C. You may elect any number of multiples for Option B and Option C as long as the total number of multiples for each option does not exceed 5.

You may also enroll during a FEGLI Open Season, which is held infrequently. You will receive plenty of notice when there is a FEGLI Open Season. The most recent FEGLI Open Seasons were held in 2004 and in 1999.

How do I enroll?

You may be able to enroll using the Life Insurance Election Form (Standard Form 2817) or through an agency self-service system such as EBIS. Contact the human resources office of your employing agency for details on how you can enroll.

Who gets the benefits paid after my death?

When you die, the Office of Federal Employees' Group Life Insurance (OFEGLI), an administrative unit of Metropolitan Life Insurance Company (MetLife), will pay life insurance benefits in a particular order set by law. The FEGLI Program Booklet, available from your human resources office and at www.opm.gov/insure/life, contains more details.

How does my beneficiary file a claim?

He or she must use a specific form called the Claim for Death Benefits (FE-6) to claim FEGLI benefits, available from your human resources office or retirement system or at www.opm.gov/insure/life.

How do I get more information about this Program?

Contact your agency human resources office. If you are retired, contact OPM's Retirement Operations Center at retire@opm.gov or by calling 1-888-767-6738. Neither OFEGLI nor OPM's Insurance Operations offices maintain records for active Federal employees or retirees.

Federal Long Term Care Insurance Program (FLTCIP)

What does this Program offer?

The FLTCIP offers insurance that helps cover the costs of certain long term care services. Long term care is the assistance you receive to perform activities of daily living – such as bathing or dressing yourself – or supervision you receive because of a severe cognitive impairment, such as Alzheimer's disease. Long term care can be provided in a facility, like a nursing home, but is most often provided at home.

Key FLTCIP facts

- The FLTCIP is **not** part of the annual Federal Benefits Open Season.
- You must apply and answer questions about your health to find out if you are approved to enroll.
- You can apply for coverage at any time using the full underwriting application; you do not have to wait for an Open Season.
- New/newly eligible employees and their spouses and newly married spouses of employees can apply with abbreviated underwriting (fewer questions about their health) within 60 days of becoming eligible.
- Qualified family members including same-sex domestic partners can also apply, with full underwriting.
- Once enrolled, you can keep your coverage even if you are no longer in an eligible group (for example, you leave your job with the Federal Government).

How much does it cost?

If you are approved for coverage, your premium is based on your age on the date your application is received and on the benefit options you select. You may pay your premiums through deductions from pay or annuity, by automatic bank withdrawal, or by direct bill.

Please Note: Your premiums do not change because you get older or your health changes after your coverage becomes effective. However, premiums are not guaranteed. We may only increase premiums if you are among a group of enrollees whose premium is determined to be inadequate.

Am I eligible to apply?

Most Federal employees are eligible to apply for coverage; those who are not eligible usually have limited appointments of short duration, or work sporadically only during certain seasons or when needed by their Federal agency. If you are eligible for the FEHB Program you are eligible to apply for coverage under the FLTCIP, even if you are not enrolled in the FEHB Program. Retirees are eligible to apply.

Federal Long Term Care Insurance Program (FLTCIP)

Which family members are eligible?

Enrollment in the FLTCIP is on an individual basis. If you are eligible as a Federal employee or annuitant, your spouse, same-sex domestic partner, and your adult children at least 18 years old are eligible to apply for coverage even if you do not. If you are a Federal employee, your parents, parents-in-law, and step parents are also eligible to apply.

For more information on eligibility, visit www.ltcfeds.com/eligibility.

How do I apply?

You apply by completing an application found at www.ltcfeds.com or by calling 1-800-LTC-FEDS. You must pass a medical screening (called underwriting). Certain medical conditions, or combinations of conditions, will prevent some people from being approved for coverage. By applying while you're in good health, you could avoid the risk of having a future change in your health disqualify you from obtaining coverage. Also, the younger you are when you apply, the lower your premiums.

If you are a new or newly eligible employee, you (and your spouse, if applicable) have 60 days to apply using the abbreviated underwriting application, which asks fewer questions about your health. Newly married spouses of employees also have 60 days to apply using abbreviated underwriting. You and your qualified relatives, including same-sex domestic partners may apply anytime using the full underwriting application.

What should I consider in making my decision to participate in this Program?

Remember that FEHB plans do not cover the cost of long term care. While Medicare covers some care in nursing homes and at home, it does so only for a limited time, subject to restrictions. The need for long term care can strike anyone at any age and the cost of care can be substantial.

Be sure to visit www.ltcfeds.com for the most up-to-date information about the FLTCIP before deciding whether to apply.

How do I get more information about this Program?

Call 1-800-LTC-FEDS (1-800-582-3337), (TTY 1-800-843-3557) or visit www.ltcfeds.com.

This page intentionally left blank

Appendix A
FEHB Program Features

No waiting periods. You can use your benefits as soon as your coverage becomes effective. There are no pre-existing condition limitations even if you change plans.

A choice of coverage. You can choose Self Only coverage just for you, or Self and Family coverage for you, your spouse, and children under age 26. Under certain circumstances, your FEHB enrollment may cover your disabled child 26 years old or older who is incapable of self-support.

A choice of plans and options. The FEHB Program offers Fee-for-Service plans, plans offering a Point-of-Service product, Health Maintenance Organizations, High Deductible Health Plans, and Consumer-Driven Health Plans.

A Government contribution. The Government pays 72 percent of the average premium of all plans toward the total cost of your premium, but not more than 75 percent of the total premium for any plan.

Salary deduction. You pay your share of the premium through a payroll deduction and have the choice of doing so using pre-tax dollars.

Enrollment opportunities. Each year you can enroll or change your health plan enrollment during Open Season. Open Season runs from the Monday of the second full work week in November through the Monday of the second full work week in December. Also, Qualifying Life Events (QLEs) allow for certain types of changes throughout the year; see your human resources office or retirement system for details.

Continued group coverage. The FEHB Program offers continued FEHB coverage:

- for you and your family when you retire from Federal service (normally you need to be covered under the FEHB Program for the five years of service immediately before you retire),
- for your former spouse if you divorce and he or she has a qualifying court order (see your human resources office for more information),
- for your family if you die, or
- for you and your family when you move, transfer, go on leave without pay, or enter military service (certain rules about coverage and premium amounts apply; see your human resources office).

Coverage after FEHB ends. The FEHB Program offers temporary continuation of coverage (TCC) and conversion to non-group (private) coverage:

- for you and your family if you leave Federal service (including when you are not eligible to carry FEHB into retirement),
- for your covered child if he or she turns age 26, or
- for your former spouse if you divorce and he or she does not have a qualifying court order (see your human resources office for more information).

If you lose coverage under the FEHB Program, you should automatically receive a Certificate of Group Health Plan Coverage from the last FEHB plan to cover you. If not, the plan must give you one on request. This certificate may be important to qualify for benefits if you join a non-FEHB plan.

Appendix B
Choosing an FEHB Plan

What type of health plan is best for you?

You have some basic questions to answer about how you pay for and access medical care. Here are the different types of plans from which to choose.

Types of Plans	Choice of doctors, hospitals, pharmacies, and other providers	Specialty care	Out-of-pocket costs	Paperwork
Fee-for-Service w/PPO (Preferred Provider Organization)	You must use the plan's network to reduce your out-of-pocket costs. For BCBS Basic Option, you **must** use Preferred providers for your care to be eligible for benefits.	Referral not required to get benefits.	You pay fewer costs if you use a PPO provider than if you don't.	Some, if you don't use network providers.
Health Maintenance Organization	You generally must use the plan's network to reduce your out-of-pocket costs.	Referral generally required from primary care doctor to get benefits.	Your out-of-pocket costs are generally limited to copayments.	Little, if any.
Point-of-Service	You must use the plan's network to reduce your out-of-pocket costs. You may go outside the network but you will pay more.	Referral generally required to get maximum benefits.	You pay less if you use a network provider than if you don't.	Little, if you use the network. You have to file your own claims if you don't use the network.
Consumer-Driven Plans	You may use network and non-network providers. You will pay more by not using the network.	Referral not required to get maximum benefits from PPOs.	You will pay an annual deductible and cost-sharing. You pay less if you use the network.	Some, if you don't use network providers. You file a claim to obtain reimbursement from your HRA.
High Deductible Health Plans w/Health Savings Account (HSA) or Health Reimbursement Arrangement (HRA)	Some plans are network only, others pay something even if you do not use a network provider.	Referral not required to get maximum benefits from PPOs.	You will pay an annual deductible and cost-sharing. You pay less if you use the network.	Some, if you don't use network providers. If you have an HSA or HRA account, you may have to file a claim to obtain reimbursement.

Appendix B
Choosing an FEHB Plan

What should you consider when choosing a plan?
Having a variety of plans to choose from is a good thing, but it can make the process confusing. We have a tool on our website that will help you narrow your plan choice based on the benefits that are important to you; go to www.opm.gov/insure/health/search/plansearch.aspx. You can also find help in selecting a plan using tools provided by PlanSmartChoice and Consumer's Checkbook at www.opm.gov/insure/health/planinfo/index.asp.

Ask yourself these questions:

1. **How much does the plan cost?**
   This includes the premium you pay.

2. **What benefits does the plan cover?**
   Make sure the plan covers the services or supplies that are important to you, and know its limitations and exclusions.

3. **What are my out-of-pocket costs?**
   Does the plan charge a deductible (the amount you must first pay before the plan begins to pay benefits)? What is the copayment or coinsurance (the amount you share in the cost of the service or supply)?

4. **Who are the doctors, hospitals, and other care providers I can use?**
   Your costs are lower when you use providers who are part of the plan; these are "in-network" providers.

5. **How well does my plan provide quality care?**
   Quality care varies from plan to plan, and here are three sources for reviewing quality.

   - Member survey results – evaluations by current plan members are posted within the health plan benefit charts in this Guide.

   - Effectiveness of care – how a plan performs in preventing or treating common conditions is measured by the Healthcare Effectiveness Data and Information Set and is found at http://www.opm.gov/insure/health/hedis/2013/index.asp.

   - Accreditation – evaluations of health plans by independent accrediting organizations. Check the cover of your health plan's brochure for its accreditation level or go to http://reportcard.ncqa.org/plan/external/plansearch.aspx.

Appendix B
Choosing an FEHB Plan

Definitions

Brand name drug - A prescription drug that is protected by a patent, supplied by a single company, and marketed under the manufacturer's brand name.

Coinsurance - The amount you pay as your share for the medical services you receive, such as a doctor's visit. Coinsurance is a percentage of the plan's allowance for the service (you pay 20%, for example).

Copayment - The amount you pay as your share for the medical services you receive, such as a doctor's visit. A copayment is a fixed dollar amount (you pay $15, for example).

Deductible - The dollar amount of covered expenses an individual or family must pay before the plan begins to pay benefits. There may be separate deductibles for different types of services. For example, a plan can have a prescription drug benefit deductible separate from its calendar year deductible.

Formulary or Prescription Drug List - A list of both generic and brand name drugs, often made up of different cost-sharing levels or tiers, that are preferred by your health plan. Health plans choose drugs that are medically safe and cost effective. A team including pharmacists and physicians determines the drugs to include in the formulary.

Generic Drug - A generic medication is an equivalent of a brand name drug. A generic drug provides the same effectiveness and safety as a brand name drug and usually costs less. A generic drug may have a different color or shape than the brand name, but it must have the same active ingredients, strength, and dosage form (pill, liquid, or injection).

In-Network - You receive treatment from the doctors, clinics, health centers, hospitals, medical practices, and other providers with whom your plan has an agreement to care for its members.

Out-of-Network - You receive treatment from doctors, clinics, health centers, hospitals, and medical practices other than those with whom the plan has an agreement at additional cost. Members who receive services outside the network may pay all charges.

Premium Conversion - A program to allow Federal employees to use pre-tax dollars to pay insurance premiums to the FEHB Program. Based on Federal tax rules, employees can deduct their share of health insurance premiums from their taxable income, which reduces their taxes.

Provider - A doctor, hospital, health care practitioner, pharmacy, or health care facility.

Qualifying Life Events - An event that may allow enrollees in the FEHB Program to change their health benefits enrollment outside of an Open Season. These events also apply to employees under premium conversion and include such events as change in family status, loss of FEHB coverage due to termination or cancellation, and change in employment status.

Additional definitions are located at the beginning of the sections introducing the different types of health plans.

Appendix C
Qualifying Life Events (QLEs)
that May Permit You to Enroll or Change Your FEHB Enrollment

Premium Conversion allows employees who are eligible for FEHB the opportunity to pay their share of FEHB premiums with pre-tax dollars. Premium conversion plans are governed by the Internal Revenue Code, and IRS rules govern when a participant may change his or her enrollment outside of the annual Open Season. When an employee experiences a QLE, changes to the employee's FEHB enrollment may be permitted. Individuals who don't participate in Premium Conversion (employees who waived participation and retirees) may cancel their enrollment or change to Self Only at any time.

Below is a brief list of the more common QLEs. Be aware that time limits apply for requesting changes. A complete listing of QLEs can be found at www.opm.gov/forms/pdf_fill/sf2809.pdf. For more details about these and other QLEs, contact the human resources office of your employing agency.

	From Not Enrolled to Enrolled	From Self Only to Self and Family	From One Plan or Option to Another	Cancel or Change to Self Only
Change in family status that results in increase or decrease in number of eligible family members.	Yes	Yes	Yes	Yes[1]
Any change in employee's employment status that could result in entitlement to coverage.	Yes	Not Applicable	Not Applicable	Not Applicable
Employee restored to civilian position after serving in uniformed services	Yes	Yes	Yes	Yes
Employee (or covered family member) enrolled in an FEHB health maintenance organization (HMO) moves or becomes employed outside the geographic area from which the FEHB carrier accepts enrollment or, if already outside the area, moves further from this area.	Not Applicable	Yes	Yes	Not Applicable
Employee or eligible family member loses coverage under FEHB or another group insurance plan.	Yes	Yes	Yes	Yes
Enrolled employee or eligible family member gains coverage under FEHB or another group insurance plan.	No	No	No	Yes[2]

[1] *Employees may change to Self Only outside of Open Season only if the QLE caused the enrollee to be the last eligible family member under the FEHB enrollment. Employees may cancel enrollment outside of Open Season only if the QLE caused the enrollee and all eligible family members to acquire other health insurance coverage.*

[2] *Employees may change to Self Only outside of Open Season only if the QLE caused all eligible family members to acquire other health insurance coverage. Employees may cancel enrollment outside of Open Season only if the QLE caused the enrollee and all eligible family members to acquire other health insurance coverage.*

Appendix D
FEHB Member Survey Results

Each year FEHB plans with 500 or more subscribers mail the Consumers Assessment of Healthcare Providers and Systems (CAHPS)[1] to a random sample of plan members. For Health Maintenance Organizations (HMO)/Point-of-Service (POS) and High Deductible Health Plans (HDHP) and Consumer-Driven Health Plans (CDHP), the sample includes all commercial plan members, including non-Federal members. For Fee-for-Service (FFS)/Preferred Provider Organization (PPO) plans, the sample includes Federal members only. The CAHPS survey asks questions to evaluate members' satisfaction with their health plans. Independent vendors certified by the National Committee for Quality Assurance administer the surveys.

OPM reports each plan's scores on the various survey measures by showing the percentage of satisfied members on a scale of 0 to 100. Also, we list the national average for each measure. Since we offer HMO plans, FFS/PPO plans, HDHP, and CDHP plans, we compute a separate national average for each plan type.

Survey findings and member ratings are provided for the following key measures of member satisfaction:

- **Overall Plan Satisfaction** – This measure is based on the question, "Using any number from 0 to 10, where 0 is the worst health plan possible and 10 is the best health plan possible, what number would you use to rate your health plan?" We report the percentage of respondents who rated their plan 8 or higher.

- **Getting Needed Care** – How often was it easy to get an appointment, the care, tests, or treatment you thought you needed through your health plan?

- **Getting Care Quickly** – When you needed care right away, how often did you get care as soon as you thought you needed? Not counting the times you needed care right away, how often did you get an appointment at a doctor's office or clinic as soon as you thought you needed?

- **How Well Doctors Communicate** – How often did your personal doctor explain things in a way that was easy to understand? How often did your personal doctor listen carefully to you, show respect for what you had to say, and spend enough time with you?

- **Customer Service** – How often did the written materials or the Internet provide the information you needed about how your health plan works? How often did your health plan's customer service give you the information or help you needed? How often were the forms from your health plan easy to fill out?

- **Claims Processing** – How often did your health plan handle your claims quickly and correctly?

- **Plan Information on Costs** – How often were you able to find out from your health plan how much you would have to pay for a health care service or equipment, or for specific prescription drug medicines?

In evaluating plan scores, you can compare individual plan scores against other plans and against the national averages. Generally, new plans and those with fewer than 500 FEHB subscribers do not conduct CAHPS. Therefore, some of the plans listed in the Guide will not have survey data.

[1] *CAHPS is a registered trademark of the Agency for Healthcare Research and Quality (AHRQ).*

Appendix E
FEHB Plan Comparison Charts

Nationwide Fee-for-Service Plans
(Pages 34 through 36)

Fee-for-Service (FFS) plans with a Preferred Provider Organization (PPO) – A Fee-for-Service plan provides flexibility in using medical providers of your choice. You may choose medical providers who have contracted with the health plan to offer discounted charges. You may also choose medical providers who do not contract with the plan, but you will pay more of the cost.

Medical providers who have contracts with the health plan (Preferred Provider Organization or PPO) have agreed to accept the health plan's reimbursement. You usually pay a copayment or a coinsurance amount and do not file claims or other paperwork. Going to a PPO hospital does not guarantee PPO benefits for all services received in the hospital, however. Lab work, radiology, and other services from independent practitioners within the hospital are frequently not covered by the hospital's PPO agreement. If you receive treatment from medical providers who are not contracted with the health plan, you either pay them directly and submit a claim for reimbursement to the health plan or the health plan pays the provider directly according to plan coverage, and you pay a deductible, coinsurance or the balance of the billed charge. In any case, you pay a greater amount in out-of-pocket costs.

PPO-only – A PPO-only plan provides medical services only through medical providers that have contracts with the plan. With few exceptions, there is no medical coverage if you or your family members receive care from providers not contracted with the plan.

Fee-for-Service plans open only to specific groups – Several Fee-for-Service plans that are sponsored or underwritten by an employee organization strictly limit enrollment to persons who are members of that organization. If you are not certain if you are eligible, check with your human resources office first.

The Health Maintenance Organization (HMO) and Point-of-Service (POS) section begins on page 40.

The High Deductible Health Plan (HDHP) and Consumer-Driven Health Plan (CDHP) section begins on page 74 .

The tables on the following pages highlight selected features that may help you narrow your choice of health plans. The tables do not show all of your possible out-of-pocket costs. All benefits are subject to the definitions, limitations, and exclusions set forth in each plan's Federal brochure which is the official statement of benefits available under the plan's contract with the Office of Personnel Management. Always consult plan brochures before making your final decision.

Nationwide Fee-for-Service Plans

How to read this chart:

The table below highlights selected features that may help you narrow your choice of health plans. *Always consult plan brochures before making your final decision.* The chart does not show all of your possible out-of-pocket costs.

The **Deductibles** shown are the amount of covered expenses that you pay before your health plan begins to pay.

Calendar Year deductibles for families are two or more times the per person amount shown.

In some plans your combined **Prescription Drug** purchases from Mail Order and local pharmacies count toward the deductible. In other plans, only purchases from local pharmacies count. Some plans require each family member to meet a per person deductible.

The **Hospital Inpatient** deductible is what you pay each time you are admitted to a hospital.

Doctors shows what you pay for inpatient surgical services and for office visits.

Your share of **Hospital Inpatient Room and Board** covered charges is shown.

| Plan Name: Open to All | Telephone Number | Enrollment Code | | Your Share of Premium | | | |
| | | | | Monthly | | Biweekly | |
		Self only	Self & family	Self only	Self & family	Self only	Self & family
APWU Health Plan (APWU) -high	800-222-2798	471	472	132.72	300.10	61.25	138.51
Blue Cross and Blue Shield Service Benefit Plan (BCBS) -std	Local phone #	104	105	140.14	433.65	69.91	200.14
Blue Cross and Blue Shield Service Benefit Plan (BCBS) -basic	Local phone #	111	112	127.91	299.70	59.07	138.32
GEHA Benefit Plan (GEHA) -high	800-821-6136	311	312	197.51	468.86	91.16	216.40
GEHA Benefit Plan (GEHA) -std	800-821-6136	314	315	97.36	221.41	44.93	102.19
MHBP -std	800-410-7778	454	455	208.32	504.59	96.61	232.89
MHBP - Value Plan	800-410-7778	414	415	93.40	223.99	43.11	103.76
NALC -high	888-636-6252	321	322	160.84	326.04	74.15	150.48
SAMBA -high	800-638-6589	441	442	248.19	637.52	114.55	294.24
SAMBA -std	800-638-6589	444	445	131.71	302.92	60.79	139.84

Plan Name: Open Only to Specific Groups							
Compass Rose Health Plan (CRHP) -high	877-531-1158	421	432	154.57	385.19	71.34	177.78
Foreign Service Benefit Plan (FSBP) -high	202-833-4910	401	402	124.11	305.79	57.28	141.15
Panama Canal Area Benefit Plan (PCABP) -high*	800-424-8196	431	432	111.70	233.14	51.55	107.51
Rural Carrier Benefit Plan (Rural) -high	800-638-8432	381	382	186.73	311.57	67.57	143.71

Prescription Drug Payment Levels Plans use a variety of terms to define what you pay for prescription drugs such as *generic*, *brand name*, *Tier I*, *Tier II*, *Level I*, etc. The 2 to 5 payment levels that plans use follow: **Level I** includes most generic drugs, but may include some preferred brands. **Level II** may include generics and preferred brands not included in Level I. **Level III** includes all other covered drugs, with some exceptions for specialty drugs. Many plans are basing how much you pay for prescription drugs on what they are changed.

Mail Order Discounts If your plan has a Mail Order program and that program is superior to the purchase of medications at the pharmacy (e.g., you get a greater quantity or pay less through Mail Order), your plan's response is "yes." If the plan does not have a Mail Order program or it is not superior to its pharmacy benefit, the plan's response is "no."

The prescription drug copayments or coinsurances described in this chart do not represent the complete range of cost-sharing under these plans. Many plans have variations in their prescription drug benefits (e.g., you pay the greater of a dollar amount or a percentage, or you pay one amount for your first prescription and then a different amount for refills). **You must read the plan brochure for a complete description of prescription drug and all other benefits.**

Plan	Benefit Type	Deductible — Per Person (Calendar Year)	Deductible — Per Person (Prescription Drug)	Hospital Inpatient	Doctors — Office Visits	Doctors — Inpatient Surgical Services	Hospital Inpatient R&B	Prescription Drugs — Level I	Prescription Drugs — Level II / Level III	Mail Order Discounts
APWU -high	PPO	$275	None	None	$18	10%	10%	$6	25%/25%	Yes
	Non-PPO	$500	None	$500	30% + diff.	30% + diff.	30%	50%	50%/50%	Yes
BCBS -std	PPO	$350	None	$250	$30	15%	Nothing	30% (5%MACare.9)	30%(Tier2)/50%(Tier4/65%Tier3)	Yes
	Non-PPO	$350	None	$350 + 35% +	35% +	35% +	Nothing	45% +	45%/45% +	Yes
BCBS -basic	PPO	None	None	$150/day x 5	$25	$150	Nothing	$10	$40/$50Tier4/50%/$10(min)/Tier3	N/A
GEHA -high	PPO	$350	None	$100	$20	10%	Nothing	$5	35% Max $150/N/A	Yes
	Non-PPO	$350	None	$300	20%	20%	Nothing	$5	35% Max $150 +/N/A	Yes
GEHA -std	PPO	$350	None	None	$10	15%	15%	$5	50% Max $200/N/A	Yes
	Non-PPO	$350	None	None	$300	35%	35%	$5	50% Max $300 +/N/A	Yes
MHBP -std	PPO	$400	None	$200	$20	10%	Nothing	$5	30%/$200 max)/50%($200 max)	Yes
	Non-PPO	$600	None	$500	50%	20%	30%	50%	50%/50%	Yes
MHBP -Value	PPO	$600	None	None	$30	20%	20%	$10	45%/75%	Yes
	Non-PPO	$900	Not Covered	None	40%	40%	40%	Not Covered	Not Covered	Yes
NALC -high	PPO	$300	None	$200	$20	15%	Nothing	20%	50%/45%	Yes
	Non-PPO	$300	None	$150	30%	30%	30%	45% +	45% +/45% +	Yes
SAMBA -high	PPO	$300	None	$200	$30	10%	Nothing	$10	15%/($5 max)/50%($50 max)	Yes
	Non-PPO	$300	None	$300	30%	30%	50%	$10	15%/($5 max)/50%($50 max)	Yes
SAMBA -std	PPO	$350	None	$0.50 up to $450	$20	15%	Nothing	$10	25%($70 max)/35%($200 max)	Yes
	Non-PPO	$550	None	$200 up to $600	35%	35%	35%	$10	25%($70 max)/35%($200 max)	Yes

Plan	Benefit Type	Deductible — Per Person (Calendar Year)	Deductible — Per Person (Prescription Drug)	Hospital Inpatient	Doctors — Office Visits	Doctors — Inpatient Surgical Services	Hospital Inpatient R&B	Prescription Drugs — Level I	Prescription Drugs — Level II / Level III	Mail Order Discounts
CREF	PPO	$350	None	$200	$15	10%	Nothing	$5	$35/50% or $50	Yes
	Non PPO	$400	None	$400	30%	50%	50%	$5	$35/50% or $50	Yes
FSBP	PPO	$350	None	Nothing	$20	10%	Nothing	$10	25%/$50 min/NA	Yes
	Non-PPO	$500	None	$200	30%	30%	30%	$10	25%/$50 min/NA	Yes
PCABF	POS	None	None	$25	$5	Nothing	50%	20%	20%/20%	No
	FPO	None	None	$100	50%	50%	50%	20%	20%/20%	No
Rural	PPO	$350	$200	$100	$20	10%	Nothing	30%	30%/50%	Yes
	Non-PPO	$400	$350	$300	35%	35%	20%	50%	50%/50%	Yes

*The Panama Canal Area Plan provides a Point-of-Service product within the Republic of Panama.

Nationwide Fee-for-Service Plans

Member Survey results are collected, scored, and reported by an independent organization – not by the health plans. See Appendix D for a fuller explanation of each survey category.

Overall Plan Satisfaction	• How would you rate your overall experience with your health plan?
Getting Needed Care	• How often was it easy to get an appointment, the care, tests, or treatment you thought you needed through your health plan?
Getting Care Quickly	• When you needed care right away, how often did you get care as soon as you thought you needed? • Not counting the times you needed care right away, how often did you get an appointment at a doctor's office or clinic as soon as you thought you needed?
How Well Doctors Communicate	• How often did your personal doctor explain things in a way that was easy to understand? • How often did your personal doctor listen carefully to you, show respect for what you had to say, and spend enough time with you?
Customer Service	• How often did written materials or the Internet provide the information you needed about how your health plan works? • How often did your health plan's customer service give you the information or help you needed? • How often were the forms from your health plan easy to fill out?
Claims Processing	• How often did your health plan handle your claims quickly and correctly?
Plan Information on Costs	• How often were you able to find out from your health plan how much you would have to pay for a health care service or equipment, or for specific prescription drug medicines?

Member Survey Results

Plan Name: Open to All	Plan Code	Overall plan satisfaction	Getting needed care	Getting care quickly	How well doctor communicate	Customer service	Claims processing	Plan Information on Costs
FFS National Average		**80.7**	**92.1**	**91.9**	**94.8**	**90.5**	**93.3**	**72.4**
APWU Health Plan - high	47 47	78.5	91	91.4	95.6	86.4	90.4	69.5
Blue Cross and Blue Shield Service Benefit Plan - std	10 10	79.9	91.5	91	94.3	90.3	96.2	68.9
Blue Cross and Blue Shield Service Benefit Plan - basic	11	72.1	93.2	93.9	92.5	92.5	92.8	66.7
GEHA Benefit Plan - high	31 31	88.3	90.4	91.1	93.5	91.7	93.7	74.3
GEHA Benefit Plan - std	51 51	74.5	89	91.6	94.1	84	91.9	76.1
MHBP - std	45 45	83.9	92.9	93	90.4	92.8	94.3	71.5
MHBP - Value Plan	41 41	84.9	90.5	87.1	94.1	90.4	90.4	61.2
NALC - high	32 32	86.3	95	92.2	95.7	93.7	98.4	77
SAMBA - high	44 44	91.1	94.6	94.6	95.4	93.1	96.9	80.2
SAMBA - std	44 44	78.5	92.5	93.9	94.3	92.9	93.4	76

Plan Name: Open Only to Specific Groups	Plan Code	Overall plan satisfaction	Getting needed care	Getting care quickly	How well doctor communicate	Customer service	Claims processing	Plan Information on Costs
FFS National Average		**80.7**	**92.1**	**91.9**	**94.8**	**90.5**	**93.3**	**72.4**
Compass Rose Health Plan	42 42	85.1	93.7	93.9	95.2	90.3	90.5	71.4
Foreign Service Benefit Plan	40 40	76.9	93.8	90.7	93.8	89.7	90.5	70
Panama Canal Area Benefit Plan	43 43							
Rural Carrier Benefit Plan	38 38	87.6	95.4	93.1	93.7	92.3	96.6	75

56

Fee-for-Service Plans – Blue Cross and Blue Shield Service Benefit Plan – Member Survey Results for Select States

Again this year we are providing more detailed information regarding the quality of services provided by our health plans. We are including the results of the Member Satisfaction survey at the *state level* for eight local Blue Cross Blue Shield (BCBS) Plans.

Plan Name	Location	Plan Code	Member Survey Results						
			Overall plan satisfaction	Getting needed care	Getting care quickly	How well doctors communicate	Customer service	Claims processing	Plan Information on Costs
FFS National Average			**80.7**	**92.1**	**91.9**	**94.8**	**90.5**	**93.3**	**72.4**
Blue Cross and Blue Shield Service - Standard	Arizona	10	86.3	90.6	89.5	92.9	91.2	95.3	74
Benefit Plan - Basic		11	79	90.5	86.6	92	91.8	96	68.6
Blue Cross and Blue Shield Service - Standard	California	10	84.7	91.9	89.4	93.7	89.7	93.7	66.4
Benefit Plan - Basic		11	72.5	87	87.5	92.3	88.9	92.6	65.1
Blue Cross and Blue Shield Service - Standard	District of Columbia	10	76.8	89.2	88.8	93.2	83.4	89.8	66.2
Benefit Plan - Basic		11	70.3	87.4	88.6	92.1	83.6	92.4	62
Blue Cross and Blue Shield Service - Standard	Florida	10	91.4	93.4	92.5	95.2	93.7	95.8	75.3
Benefit Plan - Basic		11	77.4	90.2	86.5	93.2	88.2	94.5	67.3
Blue Cross and Blue Shield Service - Standard	Illinois	10	84.3	91.3	92.3	94.7	89.5	95.3	71.1
Benefit Plan - Basic		11	78.2	91.9	89.3	94.4	88.8	95.1	66
Blue Cross and Blue Shield Service - Standard	Maryland	10	84.1	93.5	92.3	94.1	85.9	91	72.6
Benefit Plan - Basic		11	74.4	91.6	87.2	94.6	89.1	94.7	65.1
Blue Cross and Blue Shield Service - Standard	Texas	10	90.2	92.6	90.8	95.8	88.7	98	72
Benefit Plan - Basic		11	81.7	91.9	90.5	94.6	81.7	91	68.6
Blue Cross and Blue Shield Service - Standard	Virginia	10	86.8	92.6	91.8	94.9	89.4	95.7	73.6
Benefit Plan - Basic		11	79.8	91.7	92.8	94.3	89.4	96.3	67.8

The tables on the following pages highlight selected features that may help you narrow your choice of health plans. The tables do not show all of your possible out-of-pocket costs. All benefits are subject to the definitions, limitations, and exclusions set forth in each plan's Federal brochure which is the official statement of benefits available under the plan's contract with the Office of Personnel Management. Always consult plan brochures before making your final decision.

Appendix E
FEHB Plan Comparison Charts

Health Maintenance Organization Plans and Plans Offering a Point-of-Service Product
(Pages 40 through 69)

Health Maintenance Organization (HMO) – A Health Maintenance Organization provides care through a network of physicians and hospitals in particular geographic or service areas. HMOs coordinate the health care service you receive and free you from completing paperwork or being billed for covered services. Your eligibility to enroll in an HMO is determined by where you live or, for some plans, where you work.

- The HMO provides a comprehensive set of services – as long as you use the doctors and hospitals affiliated with the HMO. HMOs charge a copayment for primary physician and specialist visits and sometimes a copayment for in-hospital care.

- Most HMOs ask you to choose a doctor or medical group as your primary care physician (PCP). Your PCP provides your general medical care. In many HMOs, you must get authorization or a "referral" from your PCP to see other providers. The referral is a recommendation by your physician for you to be evaluated and/or treated by a different physician or medical professional. The referral ensures that you see the right provider for the care appropriate to your condition.

- Medical care from a provider not in the plan's network is not covered unless it's emergency care or your plan has an arrangement with another plan.

Plans Offering a Point-of-Service (POS) Product – A Point-of-Service plan is like having two plans in one – an HMO and an FFS plan. A POS allows you and your family members to choose between using, (1) a network of providers in a designated service area (like an HMO), or (2) Out-of-Network providers (like an FFS plan). When you use the POS network of providers, you usually pay a copayment for services and do not have to file claims or other paperwork. If you use non-HMO or non-POS providers, you pay a deductible, coinsurance, or the balance of the billed charge. In any case, your out-of-pocket costs are higher and you file your own claims for reimbursement.

The tables on the following pages highlight what you are expected to pay for selected features under each plan. *Always consult plan brochures before making your final decision.*

Primary care/Specialist office visit copay – Shows what you pay for each office visit to your primary care doctor and specialist. Contact your plan to find out what providers it considers specialists.

Hospital per stay deductible – Shows the amount you pay when you are admitted into a hospital.

Prescription drugs – Plans use a variety of terms to define what you pay for prescription drugs such as generic, brand, Level I, Level II, Tier I, Tier II, etc. In capturing these differences we use the following: **Level I** includes most generic drugs, but may include some preferred brands. **Level II** may include generics and preferred brands not included in Level I. **Level III** includes all other covered drugs with some exceptions for specialty drugs. The level in which a medication is placed and what you pay for prescription drugs is often based on what the plan is charged.

Mail Order Discount – If your plan has a mail order program and that program is superior to the purchase of medications at the pharmacy (e.g., you get a greater quantity or pay less through mail order), your plan's response is "yes." If the plan does not have a mail order program or it is not superior to its pharmacy benefit, the plan's response is "no."

Member Survey Results – See Appendix D for a description.

Health Maintenance Organization (HMO) and Point-of-Service (POS) Plans

See page 39 for an explanation of the columns on these pages.

Plan Name – Location	Telephone Number	Enrollment Code		Your Share of Premium			
				Monthly		Biweekly	
		Self only	Self & family	Self only	Self & family	Self only	Self & family
Alabama							
Aetna Value Plan-Most of Alabama	877-459-6604	F54	F55	124.37	282.43	57.40	130.35
Arizona							
Aetna Value Plan-All of Arizona	877-459-6604	G54	G55	122.12	277.32	56.36	127.99
Aetna Open Access-High-Phoenix and Tucson Areas	877-459-6604	WQ1	WQ2	224.96	623.15	103.83	287.61
Health Net of Arizona, Inc. -high- Maricopa/Pima/Other AZ counties	800-289-2818	A71	A72	214.19	668.30	98.86	308.45
Health Net of Arizona, Inc. -std- Maricopa/Pima/Other AZ counties	800-289-2818	A74	A75	131.09	406.72	60.50	187.72
Arkansas							
Aetna Value Plan - Most of Arkansas	877-459-6604	F54	F55	124.37	282.43	57.40	130.35
QualChoice - high - All of Arkansas	800-235-7017	DH1	DH2	180.07	469.23	83.11	216.57
QualChoice - std - All of Arkansas	800-235-7017	DH4	DH5	115.73	271.02	53.41	125.08
California							
Aetna HMO - Los Angeles and San Diego Areas	877-459-6604	2X1	2X2	148.31	389.71	68.45	179.87
Anthem Blue Cross Select HMO - High - Southern California	800-235-8631	B31	B32	152.16	368.96	70.23	170.29
Blue Shield of CA Access+HMO -high- Southern Region	800-880-8086	SI1	SI2	141.07	327.08	65.11	150.96
Health Net of California -high- Northern Region	800-522-0088	LB1	LB2	610.00	1445.64	281.54	667.22
Health Net of California -std- Northern Region	800-522-0088	LB4	LB5	561.25	1332.95	259.04	615.21
Health Net of California -high- Southern Region	800-522-0088	LP1	LP2	270.01	659.57	124.62	304.42
Health Net of California -std- Southern Region	800-522-0088	LP4	LP5	237.46	584.32	109.60	269.69
Kaiser Foundation Health Plan of California -high- Northern California	800-464-4000	591	592	316.50	821.83	146.08	379.31
Kaiser Foundation Health Plan of California -std- Northern California	800-464-4000	594	595	199.96	514.75	92.29	237.58
Kaiser Foundation Health Plan of California -high- Southern California	800-464-4000	621	622	129.55	299.42	59.79	138.19
Kaiser Foundation Health Plan of California -std- Southern California	800-464-4000	624	625	83.01	191.87	38.31	88.56
UnitedHealthcare of California -high- Central and Southern California	866-546-0510	CY1	CY2	144.02	353.27	66.47	163.05
UnitedHealthcare of California -std- Central and Southern California	866-546-0510	CY4	CY5	118.82	271.66	54.84	125.38

The information contained in this Guide is not the official statement of benefits. Each plan's Federal brochure is the official statement of benefits.

| Plan Name – Location | Primary care/ Specialist office copay | Hospital per stay deductible | Prescription Drugs | | | Member Survey Results | | | | | | |
			Level I	Level II/ Level III	Mail order discount	Overall plan satisfaction	Getting needed care	Getting care quickly	How well doctors communicate	Customer service	Claims processing	Plan Information on Costs
HMO/POS National Average						67.7	85	85.4	93.5	85.2	87.7	66.4
Alabama												
Aetna Value Plan	$25/$40	20%	$10	30%/50%	Yes							
Arizona												
Aetna Value Plan	$25/$40	20%	$10	30%/50%	Yes							
Aetna Open Access-High	$20/$35	$250/day x 4	$10	$35/$65	Yes	60.5	82.6	82.9	90.1	87.2	90.7	62.7
Health Net of Arizona, Inc.-High	$20/$40	$200/day x 5	$10	$30/50%	Yes	73.2	87.6	85.2	92.8	84.6	93.5	70.7
Health Net of Arizona, Inc.-Std	$25/$50	25%	$10	$40/50%	Yes	73.2	87.6	85.2	92.8	84.6	93.5	70.7
Arkansas												
Aetna Value Plan	$25/$40	20%	$10	30%/50%	Yes							
QualChoice-In-Network	$20/$30	$100max$500	$0	$40/$60	Yes							
QualChoice-Out-Network	40%/40%	40%	N/A	N/A	No							
QualChoice- In-Network	$20/$40	$200max$1,000	$5	$40/$60	Yes							
California												
Aetna Open Access-High	$20/$35	$250/day x 4	$10	$35/$65	Yes	59.6	72.6	77.8	88.8	82.4	88.2	58.8
Anthem Blue Cross Blue Shield HMO-High	$25/$35	None	$5,$40,$60	$5,$40,$60 /$60	Yes							
Blue Shield of CA Access+HMO-High	$20/$30	$150/day x 3	$10	$35/$50	Yes	73.6	82.8	86.2	91.9	87	84.8	65.3
Health Net of California-High	$20/$30	$150/day x 5	$10	$35/$60	Yes	66.2	83.2	79.4	90.9	81.5	83.3	65
Health Net of California-Std	$30/$50	$750	$15	$35/$65	Yes	66.2	83.2	79.4	90.9	81.5	83.3	65
Health Net of California-High	$20/$30	$150/day x 5	$10	$35/$60	Yes	66.2	83.2	79.4	90.9	81.5	83.3	65
Health Net of California-Std	$30/$50	$750	$15	$35/$65	Yes	66.2	83.2	79.4	90.9	81.5	83.3	65
Kaiser Foundation HP of California -High	$15/$25	$250	$10	$30/$30	Yes	77.8	86.6	85.7	92.1	84	74.2	62.2
Kaiser Foundation HP of California -Std	$20/$40	$500	$15	$35/$35	Yes	77.8	86.6	85.7	92.1	84	74.2	62.2
Kaiser Foundation HP of California -High	$10/$20	$250	$10	$30/$30	Yes	82.5	82.4	78.2	93.2	83.8	82.4	70.2
Kaiser Foundation HP of California -Std	$20/$40	$500	$15	$35/$35	Yes	82.5	82.4	78.2	93.2	83.8	82.4	70.2
United Healthcare of California -High	$20/$35	$150/day x 4	$10	$35/$60	Yes	65.3	79.7	78.1	89.9	77.6	86.9	59.9
United Healthcare of California -Standard	$25/$40	30%	$10	$25/$50	Yes							

Health Maintenance Organization (HMO) and Point-of-Service (POS) Plans

See page 39 for an explanation of the columns on these pages.

Plan Name – Location	Telephone Number	Enrollment Code		Your Share of Premium					
				Monthly		Biweekly			
		Self only	Self & family	Self only	Self & family	Self only	Self & family		
Colorado									
Aetna Value Plan - All of Colorado	877-459-6604	G54	G55	122.12	277.32	56.36	127.99		
Kaiser Foundation Health Plan of Colorado -high- Denver/Boulder/Southern Colorado areas	800-632-9700	651	652	196.02	456.77	90.47	210.82		
Kaiser Foundation Health Plan of Colorado -std- Denver/Boulder/Southern Colorado areas	800-632-9700	654	655	90.35	204.19	41.70	94.24		
Connecticut									
Aetna Value Plan - All of Connecticut	877-459-6604	EP4	EP5	120.89	274.54	55.80	126.71		
Delaware									
Aetna Value Plan - All of Delaware	877-459-6604	EP4	EP5	120.89	274.54	55.80	126.71		
Aetna Open Access -High- Kent/New Castle/Sussex areas	877-459-6604	P31	P32	668.00	1688.74	308.31	779.42		
Aetna Open Access -Basic- Kent/New Castle/Sussex areas	877-459-6604	P34	P35	392.75	940.98	181.27	434.30		
District of Columbia									
Aetna Value Plan - All of Washington, D.C.	877-459-6604	F54	F55	124.37	282.43	57.40	130.35		
Aetna Open Access -high- Washington, DC Area	877-459-6604	JN1	JN2	436.06	982.17	201.26	453.31		
Aetna Open Access -basic- Washington, DC Area	877-459-6604	JN4	JN5	133.79	304.25	61.75	140.42		
CareFirst BlueChoice -high- Washington, D.C. Metro Area	888-789-9065	2G1	2G2	156.08	360.62	72.04	166.44		
CareFirst BlueChoice -std- Washington, D.C. Metro Area	888-789-9065	2G4	2G5	135.27	304.32	62.43	140.45		
Kaiser Foundation Health Plan Mid-Atlantic States -high- Washington, DC area	877-574-3337	E31	E32	152.81	381.76	70.53	176.20		
Kaiser Foundation Health Plan Mid-Atlantic States -std- Washington, DC area	877-574-3337	E34	E35	94.45	217.24	43.59	100.26		
M.D. IPA -high- Washington, DC area	877-835-9861	JP1	JP2	166.96	417.79	77.06	192.83		

The information contained in this Guide is not the official statement of benefits. Each plan's Federal brochure is the official statement of benefits.

Plan Name – Location	Primary care/ Specialist office copay	Hospital per stay deductible	Prescription Drugs			Member Survey Results						
			Level I	Level II/ Level III	Mail order discount	Overall plan satisfaction	Getting needed care	Getting care quickly	How well doctors communicate	Customer service	Claims processing	Plan Information on Costs
HMO/POS National Average						67.7	85	85.4	93.5	85.2	87.7	66.4
Colorado												
Aetna Value Plan	$25/$40	20%	$10	30%/50%	Yes							
Kaiser Foundation HP of Colorado -High	$20/$40	$250	$10	$35/$60	Yes	70.8	84.3	84.3	93.5	80.1	81.4	67.1
Kaiser Foundation HP of Colorado -Std	$25/$45	10%	$15	$40/$80	Yes	70.8	84.3	84.3	93.5	80.1	81.4	67.1
Connecticut												
Aetna Value Plan	$25/$40	20%	$10	30%/50%	Yes							
Delaware												
Aetna Value Plan	$25/$40	20%	$10	30%/50%	Yes							
Aetna Open Access-High	$20/$35	$250/day x 4	$10	$35/$65	Yes	66.3	83.3	85.2	92.9	84.7	89.8	63.8
Aetna Open Access-Basic	$15/$35	20% Plan Allow	$5	$35/$65	Yes	66.3	83.3	85.2	92.9	84.7	89.8	63.8
District of Columbia												
Aetna Value Plan	$25/$40	20%	$10	30%/50%	Yes							
Aetna Open Access-High	$15/$30	$150/day x 3	$5	$35/$65	Yes	64.9	84.7	85.2	94.3	89.1	85.7	62.1
Aetna Open Access-Basic	$20/$35	10% Plan Allow	$10	$35/$65	Yes	64.9	84.7	85.2	94.3	89.1	85.7	62.1
CareFirst BlueChoice-High	$25/$35	$200	Nothing	$30/$50	Yes	63.1	84.3	87.3	91.5	79.8	85.9	55.8
CareFirst BlueChoice-In-Network	Nothing/$35	$200	Nothing	$30/$50	Yes	63.1	84.3	87.3	91.5	79.8	85.9	55.8
CareFirst BlueChoice-Out-Network	$70/$70	$500	Nothing	$30/$50	Yes	63.1	84.3	87.3	91.5	79.8	85.9	55.8
Kaiser Foundation HP Mid-Atlantic States -High	$10/$20	$100	$7/$17 Net	$30/$50/$45/$65	Yes	77.8	84.7	85.4	93.2	83.5	75.8	69.6
Kaiser Foundation HP Mid-Atlantic States -Std	$20/$30	$250/day x 3	$12/$22Net	$35/$55/$50/$70	Yes	77.8	84.7	85.4	93.2	83.5	75.8	69.6
M.D. IPA-High	$25/$40	$150/day x 3	$7	$30/$60	Yes	57.4	83.5	88.1	92.3	86.1	87.2	67.9

Health Maintenance Organization (HMO) and Point-of-Service (POS) Plans

See page 39 for an explanation of the columns on these pages.

Plan Name – Location	Telephone Number	Enrollment Code		Your Share of Premium			
				Monthly		Biweekly	
		Self only	Self & family	Self only	Self & family	Self only	Self & family
Florida							
Aetna Value Plan - Most of Florida	877-459-6604	F54	F55	124.37	282.43	57.40	130.35
AvMed Health Plan -high- Broward, Dade and Palm Beach	800-882-8633	ML1	ML2	225.07	611.91	103.88	282.42
AvMed Health Plan -std- Broward, Dade and Palm Beach	800-882-8633	ML4	ML5	126.10	302.66	58.20	139.69
Capital Health Plan -high- Tallahassee area	850-383-3311	EA1	EA2	108.88	288.56	50.25	133.18
Coventry Health Plan of Florida -high- Southern Florida	800-441-5501	5E1	5E2	155.56	445.05	71.80	205.41
Coventry Health Plan of Florida -std- Southern Florida	800-441-5501	5E4	5E5	130.40	426.96	60.18	197.06
Humana Medical Plan, Inc. -high- South Florida	888-393-6765	EE1	EE2	184.79	410.43	85.29	189.43
Humana Medical Plan, Inc. -std- South Florida	888-393-6765	EE4	EE5	123.15	274.02	56.84	126.47
Humana Medical Plan, Inc. -high- Tampa	888-393-6765	LL1	LL2	400.92	891.52	185.04	411.38
Humana Medical Plan, Inc. -std- Tampa	888-393-6765	LL4	LL5	136.84	304.46	63.16	140.52
Georgia							
Aetna Value Plan - All of Georgia	877-459-6604	F54	F55	124.37	282.43	57.40	130.35
Aetna Open Access -high- Atlanta and Athens Areas	877-459-6604	2U1	2U2	379.19	898.19	175.01	414.55
Humana Employers Health of Georgia, Inc. -high- Columbus	888-393-6765	CB1	CB2	136.84	304.46	63.16	140.52
Humana Employers Health of Georgia, Inc. -std- Columbus	888-393-6765	CB4	CB5	129.31	287.72	59.68	132.79
Humana Employers Health of Georgia, Inc. -high- Atlanta	888-393-6765	DG1	DG2	136.84	304.46	63.16	140.52
Humana Employers Health of Georgia, Inc. -std- Atlanta	888-393-6765	DG4	DG5	130.30	289.92	60.14	133.81
Humana Employers Health of Georgia, Inc. -high- Macon	888-393-6765	DN1	DN2	136.84	304.46	63.16	140.52
Humana Employers Health of Georgia, Inc. -std- Macon	888-393-6765	DN4	DN5	129.31	287.72	59.68	132.79
Kaiser Foundation Health Plan of Georgia -high- Atlanta, Athens, Columbus, Macon, Savannah	888-865-5813	F81	F82	138.08	339.60	63.73	156.74
Kaiser Foundation Health Plan of Georgia -std- Atlanta, Athens, Columbus, Macon, Savannah	888-865-5813	F84	F85	96.57	220.67	44.57	101.85
Guam							
Calvo's Selectcare-High- Guam, Northern Mariana Islands, Palau	671-479-7982	B41	B42	133.28	480.24	61.51	221.65
TakeCare -high- Guam/N.Mariana Islands/Belau(Palau)	671-647-3526	JK1	JK2	124.47	387.63	57.45	178.91
TakeCare -std- Guam/N.Mariana Islands/Belau(Palau)	671-647-3526	JK4	JK5	109.56	289.52	50.57	133.53

The information contained in this Guide is not the official statement of benefits. Each plan's Federal brochure is the official statement of benefits.

Plan Name – Location	Primary care/Specialist office copay	Hospital per stay deductible	Prescription Drugs			Member Survey Results						
			Level I	Level II/Level III	Mail order discount	Overall plan satisfaction	Getting needed care	Getting care quickly	How well doctors communicate	Customer service	Claims processing	Plan Information on Costs
HMO/POS National Average						67.7	85	85.4	93.5	85.2	87.7	66.4
Florida												
Aetna Value Plan	$25/$40	20%	$10	30%/50%	Yes							
AvMed Health Plans-High	$15/$40	$150/day x 5	$5	$30/$50/30%	No	74.4	82	82.4	93.9	89.5	92.5	68.9
AvMed Health Plans-Std	$25/$45	$175/day x 5	$10	$40/$60/30%	No	74.4	82	82.4	93.9	89.5	92.5	68.9
Capital Health Plan-High	$15/$25	$250	$15 Tier 1	$30Tier2/$50Tier3	No	84.4	92.7	91.7	94.5	88.9	94.4	76.5
Coventry Health Plan of Florida-High	$15/$30	Ded+$150x3	$3/$20	$40/$60/20%	No	46.3	79.3	77.7	86.9	81.6	73.9	59.9
Coventry Health Plan of Florida-Standard	$20/$50	Ded+$150x5	$3/$10	$50/$70/20%	No	46.3	79.3	77.7	86.9	81.6	73.9	59.9
Humana Medical Plan, Inc.-High	$20/$35	$250/day x 3	$10	$40/$60	Yes	61.3	82.7	83.5	94.6	85	82.8	68.9
Humana Medical Plan, Inc.-Standard	$25/$40	$500/day x 3	$10	$40/$60	Yes	61.3	82.7	83.5	94.6	85	82.8	68.9
Humana Medical Plan, Inc. -High	$20/$35	$250/day x 3	$10	$40/$60	Yes							
Humana Medical Plan, Inc. -Standard	$25/$40	$500/day x 3	$10	$40/$60	Yes							
Georgia												
Aetna Value Plan	$25/$40	20%	$10	30%/50%	Yes							
Aetna Open Access-High	$20/$35	$250/day x 4	$10	$35/$65	Yes	61.4	86.7	84.3	92	82.9	87	59.9
Humana Employers Health of Georgia, Inc.-High	$20/$35	$250/day x 3	$10	$40/$60	Yes							
Humana Employers Health of Georgia, Inc.-Std	$25/$40	$500/day x 3	$10	$40/$60	Yes							
Humana Employers Health of Georgia, Inc.-High	$20/$35	$250/day x 3	$10	$40/$60	Yes	52.8	87.3	86.7	95.4	77.1	86.4	56.6
Humana Employers Health of Georgia, Inc.-Std	$25/$40	$500/day x 3	$10	$40/$60	Yes	52.8	87.3	86.7	95.4	77.1	86.4	56.6
Humana Employers Health of Georgia, Inc.-High	$20/$35	$250/day x 3	$10	$40/$60	Yes							
Humana Employers Health of Georgia, Inc.-Std	$25/$40	$500/day x 3	$10	$40/$60	Yes							
Kaiser Foundation HP of Georgia -High	$15/$30	$250 day x 5	$10/$20 Comm	$40/$50 Comm	Yes	78	82.2	84.2	92.9	85.8	87.4	64.7
Kaiser Foundation HP of Georgia -Std	$20/$35	$250/day x 5	$15/$25 Comm	$40/$50 Comm	Yes	78	82.2	84.2	92.9	85.8	87.4	64.7
Guam												
Calvo's Selectcare-In-Network	$15/$40	$200	$10	$25/50%/$40PP	Yes							
Calvo's Selectcare-Out-Network	30%/30%	30%	N/A	N/A	No							
TakeCare-High	$15at FHP/$40	$100/day for 5 days	$10	$10/$25/$50	No	67.9	75.1	73.1	90.7	76.2	71.3	60.3
TakeCare-Std	$15/$40	$150/day for 5 days	$15	$15/$40/$80	No	67.9	75.1	73.1	90.7	76.2	71.3	60.3

Health Maintenance Organization (HMO) and Point-of-Service (POS) Plans

See page 39 for an explanation of the columns on these pages.

| Plan Name – Location | Telephone Number | Enrollment Code | | Your Share of Premium | | | |
| | | | | Monthly | | Biweekly | |
		Self only	Self & family	Self only	Self & family	Self only	Self & family
Hawaii							
HMSA -high- All of Hawaii	800-776-4622	871	872	114.92	255.81	53.04	118.06
Kaiser Foundation Health Plan of Hawaii -high- Hawaii/Kauai/Lanai/Maui/Molokai/Oahu	808-432-5955	631	632	135.51	302.20	62.54	139.48
Kaiser Foundation Health Plan of Hawaii -std- Hawaii/Kauai/Lanai/Maui/Molokai/Oahu	808-432-5955	634	635	69.60	155.22	32.12	71.64
Idaho							
Aetna Value Plan - Most of Idaho	877-459-6604	H44	H45	124.69	283.17	57.55	130.69
Altius Health Plans -high- Southern Region	800-377-4161	9K1	9K2	210.84	452.87	97.31	209.02
Altius Health Plans -std- Southern Region	800-377-4161	DK4	DK5	112.90	248.37	52.11	114.63
Group Health Cooperative -high- most of Washington State & Northern Idaho	888-901-4636	541	542	242.01	488.64	111.70	225.53
Group Health Cooperative -std- most of Washington State & Northern Idaho	888-901-4636	544	545	105.37	237.90	48.63	109.80
SelectHealth-High-Utah, Idaho	801-538-5038	SF1	SF2	204.75	458.40	94.50	211.57
SelectHealth-Std-Utah, Idaho	801-538-5038	SF4	SF5	139.21	312.19	64.25	144.09
Illinois							
Aetna Value Plan - Most of Illinois	877-459-6604	H44	H45	124.69	283.17	57.55	130.69
Blue Cross and Blue Shield of Illinois-High-Illinois	800-892-2803	A21	A22	279.84	653.22	129.16	301.49
Blue Preferred Plus POS -high- Madison and St. Clair counties	888-811-2092	9G1	9G2	284.29	590.00	131.21	272.31
Health Alliance HMO -high- Central/E.Central/N. Cent/South/West	800-851-3379	FX1	FX2	281.97	700.39	130.14	323.26
Humana Benefit Plan of Illinois, Inc. -high- Central and Northwestern	888-393-6765	9F1	9F2	422.76	939.94	195.12	433.82
Humana Benefit Plan of Illinois, Inc. -std- Central and Northwestern	888-393-6765	AB4	AB5	136.84	304.46	63.16	140.52
Humana Health Plan Inc. -high- Chicago	888-393-6765	751	752	336.89	748.88	155.49	345.64
Humana Health Plan Inc. -std- Chicago	888-393-6765	754	755	136.83	304.46	63.15	140.52
Union Health Service -high- Chicago area	312-423-4200	761	762	129.27	297.31	59.66	137.22
United Healthcare of the Midwest -high- Southwest Illinois	877-835-9861	B91	B92	214.02	481.17	98.78	222.08
United Healthcare Plan of the River Valley Inc. -high- West Central Illinois	800-747-1446	YH1	YH2	142.17	391.92	65.62	180.89

The information contained in this Guide is not the official statement of benefits. Each plan's Federal brochure is the official statement of benefits.

Plan Name – Location	Primary care/ Specialist office copay	Hospital per stay deductible	Prescription Drugs			Member Survey Results						
			Level I	Level II/ Level III	Mail order discount	Overall plan satisfaction	Getting needed care	Getting care quickly	How well doctors communicate	Customer service	Claims processing	Plan Information on Costs
HMO/POS National Average						67.7	85	85.4	93.5	85.2	87.7	66.4
Hawaii												
HMSA-In-Network	$15/$15	$100	$7	$30/$65	Yes	88.1	91.3	88.9	95.2	85.7	94.4	64.2
HMSA-Out-Network	30%/30%	30%	$7 + 20%	$30+20%/$65+20%	No	88.1	91.3	88.9	95.2	85.7	94.4	64.2
Kaiser Foundation HP of Hawaii -High	$20/$20	$100	$15	$15/$15	Yes	75.7	80.2	80.7	93.6	79.4	87.1	67.6
Kaiser Foundation HP of Hawaii -Std	$30/$30	10%	$20	$20/$20	Yes	75.7	80.2	80.7	93.6	79.4	87.1	67.6
Idaho												
Aetna Value Plan	$25/$40	20%	$10	30%/50%	Yes							
Altius Health Plans-High	$20/$30	$200	$7	$25/$50	Yes	60.8	86.5	89.6	94.7	82.1	88.3	60.7
Altius Health Plans-Std	$20/$35	None	$7	$35/$60	Yes	60.8	86.5	89.6	94.7	82.1	88.3	60.7
Group Health Cooperative-High	$25/$25	$350/day x 3	$20	$40/$60	Yes	70.9	82.8	86.2	92.1	85.5	91.5	71.3
Group Health Cooperative-Std	4/$25-$25+20%	$500/day x 3	$20	$40/$60	Yes	70.9	82.8	86.2	92.1	85.5	91.5	71.3
SelectHealth-High	$15/$25	$100	$5	$25/$50	Yes							
SelectHealth-Standard	$20/$30	$100 after ded	$5,$25,$50	$25/$50/$50	Yes							
Illinois												
Aetna Value Plan	$25/$40	20%	$10	30%/50%	Yes							
Blue Cross and Blue Shield of Illinois-High	$20/$35	None	$10 copay	$40/$60	Yes							
Blue Preferred Plus POS-In-Network	$25/$35	$500	$10	$30/$50/25%/$50/25%	Yes	64.7	89.6	87.5	93.6	82.6	91.1	63.9
Blue Preferred Plus POS-Out-Network	30% after ded.	30% after ded.	N/A	N/A	No	64.7	89.6	87.5	93.6	82.6	91.1	63.9
Health Alliance HMO-High	$25/$50	$200/day up to $5	$7	$35/$70	Yes	82.3	89.6	88.8	97.3	92.2	88.1	70.9
Humana Benefit Plan of Illinois Inc. -High	$20/$35	$250/day x 3	$10	$40/$60	Yes	56.5	84.1	85.1	91	75.5	73.9	67.8
Humana Benefit Plan of Illinois Inc. -Std	$25/$40	$500/day X 3	$10	$40/$60	Yes	56.5	84.1	85.1	91	75.5	73.9	67.8
Humana Health Plan, Inc. -High	$20/$35	$250/day x 3	$10	$40/$60	Yes	62.1	80.9	77.9	90.9	83	82.3	68.5
Humana Health Plan, Inc. -Std	$25/$40	$500/day x 3	$10	$40/$60	Yes	62.1	80.9	77.9	90.9	83	82.3	68.5
Union Health Service -High	$15/$15	None	$10	$35/$60	No							
UHC of the Midwest, Inc. -High	$25/$40	$450	$7	$30/$60	Yes	71.4	91.1	89.4	96.7	87.9	92	69.5
UHC Plan of the River Valley, Inc. -High	$20/$50	Nothing	$10	$35/$50	Yes	53.5	86.7	85.4	96.2	83	90.4	59.9

Health Maintenance Organization (HMO) and Point-of-Service (POS) Plans

See page 39 for an explanation of the columns on these pages.

| Plan Name – Location | Telephone Number | Enrollment Code | | Your Share of Premium | | | |
| | | | | Monthly | | Biweekly | |
		Self only	Self & family	Self only	Self & family	Self only	Self & family
Indiana							
Health Alliance HMO -high- Western Indiana	800-851-3379	FX1	FX2	281.97	700.39	130.14	323.26
Humana Health Plan of Ohio -high-Portions of Indiana	888-393-6765	A61	A62	129.99	289.24	60.00	133.49
Humana Health Plan of Ohio -std-Portions of Indiana	888-393-6765	A64	A65	116.99	260.31	54.00	120.14
Humana Health Plan Inc. -high- Lake/Porter/LaPorte Counties	888-393-6765	751	752	336.89	748.88	155.49	345.64
Humana Health Plan Inc. -std- Lake/Porter/LaPorte Counties	888-393-6765	754	755	136.83	304.46	63.15	140.52
Humana Health Plan Inc. -high- Southern Indiana	888-393-6765	MH1	MH2	136.84	304.46	63.16	140.52
Humana Health Plan Inc. -std- Southern Indiana	888-393-6765	MH4	MH5	129.99	289.23	59.99	133.49
Physicians Health Plan of Northern Indiana -high- Northeast Indiana	260-432-6690	DQ1	DQ2	253.84	564.65	117.16	260.61
Iowa							
Aetna Value Plan - All of Iowa	877-459-6604	H44	H45	124.69	283.17	57.55	130.69
Coventry Health Care of Iowa -high- Central/Eastern/Western Iowa	800-257-4692	SV1	SV2	130.10	346.45	60.05	159.90
Coventry Health Care of Iowa -std- Central/Eastern/Western Iowa	800-257-4692	SY4	SY5	95.95	225.49	44.28	104.07
Health Alliance HMO -high- Central Iowa	800-851-3379	FX1	FX2	281.97	700.39	130.14	323.26
HealthPartners -high-Option-Northern Iwoa	800-883-2177	V31	V32	317.83	761.30	146.69	351.37
HealthPartners -std-Option-Northern Iowa	800-883-2177	V34	V35	89.87	206.71	41.48	95.40
Sanford Health Plan -high- Northwestern Iowa	800-752-5863	AU1	AU2	243.18	590.13	112.24	272.37
Sanford Health Plan -std- Northwestern Iowa	800-752-5863	AU4	AU5	218.03	531.80	100.63	245.45
UnitedHealthcare Plan of the River Valley Inc. -high- Eastern and Central Iowa	800-747-1446	YH1	YH2	142.17	391.92	65.62	180.89
Kansas							
Aetna Value Plan - Most of Kansas	877-459-6604	G54	G55	122.12	277.32	56.36	127.99
Aetna Open Access - High- Kansas City area	877-459-6604	HY1	HY2	124.05	402.76	57.25	185.89
Coventry Health Care of Kansas -high- Kansas City Metro Area (KS and MO)	800-969-3343	HA1	HA2	129.96	305.41	59.98	140.96
Coventry Health Care of Kansas -std- Kansas City Metro Area (KS and MO)	800-969-3343	HA4	HA5	109.79	258.00	50.67	119.08
Humana Health Plan, Inc. -high- Kansas City area	888-393-6765	MS1	MS2	517.61	1150.97	238.90	531.22
Humana Health Plan, Inc. -std- Kansas City area	888-393-6765	MS4	MS5	136.81	304.42	63.14	140.50

The information contained in this Guide is not the official statement of benefits. Each plan's Federal brochure is the official statement of benefits.

Plan Name – Location	Primary care/ Specialist office copay	Hospital per stay deductible	Level I	Level II/ Level III	Mail order discount	Overall plan satisfaction 6	Getting needed care	Getting care quickly	How well doctors communicate	Customer service	Claims processing	Plan Information on Costs
				HMO/POS National Average		67.7	85	85.4	93.5	85.2	87.7	66.4
Indiana												
Health Alliance HMO-High	$25/$50	Nothing	$7	$35/$70	Yes	82.3	89.6	88.8	97.3	92.2	88.1	70.9
Humana HP of Ohio-High	$20/$35	$250 x 3 days	$10	$40/$60	Yes							
Humana HP of Ohio-Std	$25/$40	$500 x 3 days	$10	$40/$60	Yes							
Humana Health Plan Inc.-High	$20/$35	$250/day x 3	$10	$40/$60	Yes	62.1	80.9	77.9	90.9	83	82.3	68.5
Humana Health Plan Inc.-Std	$25/$40	$500/day x 3	$10	$40/$60	Yes	62.1	80.9	77.9	90.9	83	82.3	68.5
Humana Health Plan Inc.-High	$20/$35	$250/day x 3	$10	$40/$60	Yes	47.2	87.2	79.6	92.9	86.6	86	65.7
Humana Health Plan Inc.-Std	$25/$40	$500/day x 3	$10	$40/$60	Yes	47.2	87.2	79.6	92.9	86.6	86	65.7
Physicians Health Plan of Northern Indiana-High	$15/$15	20%	$10	$25/$50	Yes	54.7	89.2	85.6	94.3	86.3	94.8	58.8
Iowa												
Aetna Value Plan	$25/$40	20%	$10	30%/50%	Yes							
Coventry Health Care of Iowa-High	$20/$45	20%	$3/$10	$45/$70	Yes	49	86	86.6	96	84.7	89.1	66.5
Coventry Health Care of Iowa-Std	$20/$45	20%	$3/$10	30%/5,000Max	No	49	86	86.6	96	84.7	89.1	66.5
Health Alliance HMO-High	$25/$50	$200/day up to 5	$7	$35/$70	Yes	82.3	89.6	88.8	97.3	92.2	88.1	70.9
HealthPartners-High Option	$25/$45	Nothing	$12	$45/$90	Yes	60.3	85.7	88.2	97.8	90	89.2	68.9
HealthPartners-Standard Option	$0 for 3, then 20%	20% in/40% out	$9	$40/$70	Yes	60.3	85.7	88.2	97.8	90	89.2	68.9
Sanford Health Plan-In-Network-High	$20/$30	$100/day x 5	$15	$30/$50	No	52.3	83.9	86.6	96	83.1	91	65.6
Sanford Health Plan-Out-Network-High	40%/40%	40%	40%+	40%+	No	52.3	83.9	86.6	96	83.1	91	65.6
Sanford Health Plan-In-Network-Std	$25/$25	$100/day x 5	$15	$30/$50	No	52.3	83.9	86.6	96	83.1	91	65.6
Sanford Health Plan-Out-Network-Std	40%/40%	40%	40%+	40%+	No	52.3	83.9	86.6	96	83.1	91	65.6
UHC Plan of the River Valley, Inc.-High	$25/$50	Nothing	$10	$35/$50	Yes	53.5	86.7	85.4	96.2	83	90.4	59.9
Kansas												
Aetna Value Plan	$25/$40	20%	$10	30%/50%	Yes							
Aetna Open Access-High	$20/$35	$250/day x 4	$10	$35/$65	Yes							
Coventry Health Care of Kansas-High	$25/$60	25%	$3/$12	$50/$75	Yes	59.1	87.2	87	95.8	86.7	89.2	62.9
Coventry Health Care of Kansas-Std	$30/$60	30%	$3/$12	$50/20%	Yes	59.1	87.2	87	95.8	86.7	89.2	62.9
Humana Health Plan, Inc.-High	$20/$35	$250/day x 3	$10	$40/$60	Yes	64.4	86.3	86.9	93.2	87.2	90.9	72.2
Humana Health Plan, Inc.-Std	$25/$40	$500/day x 3	$10	$40/$60	Yes	64.4	86.3	86.9	93.2	87.2	90.9	72.2

Health Maintenance Organization (HMO) and Point-of-Service (POS) Plans

See page 39 for an explanation of the columns on these pages.

Plan Name – Location	Telephone Number	Enrollment Code		Your Share of Premium			
				Monthly		Biweekly	
		Self only	Self & family	Self only	Self & family	Self only	Self & family
Kentucky							
Aetna Value Plan-Most of Kentucky	877-459-6604	H44	H45	124.69	283.17	57.55	130.69
Humana Health Plan of Ohio-High-Portions of Kentucky	888-393-6765	A61	A62	129.99	289.24	60.00	133.49
Humana Health Plan of Ohio-Std-Portions of Kentucky	888-393-6765	A64	A65	116.99	260.31	54.00	120.14
Humana Health Plan, Inc. -high- Louisville	888-393-6765	MH1	MH2	136.84	304.46	63.16	140.52
Humana Health Plan, Inc. -std- Louisville	888-393-6765	MH4	MH5	129.99	289.23	59.99	133.49
Humana Health Plan, Inc. -high- Lexington	888-393-6765	MI1	MI2	155.59	345.49	71.81	159.46
Humana Health Plan, Inc. -std- Lexington	888-393-6765	MI4	MI5	129.99	289.23	59.99	133.49
Louisiana							
Aetna Value Plan - Most of Louisiana	877-459-6604	F54	F55	124.37	282.43	57.40	130.35
Coventry Health Care of Louisiana -high- New Orleans area	800-341-6613	BJ1	BJ2	204.73	515.01	94.49	237.70
Coventry Health Care of Louisiana -std- New Orleans area	800-341-6613	BJ4	BJ5	130.35	302.71	60.16	139.71
Maine							
Aetna Value Plan-All of Maine	877-459-6604	EP4	EP5	120.89	274.54	55.80	126.71
Maryland							
Aetna Value Plan-All of Maryland	877-459-6604	F54	F55	124.37	282.43	57.40	130.35
Aetna Open Access -high- Northern/Central/Southern Maryland Areas	877-459-6604	JN1	JN2	436.06	982.17	201.26	453.51
Aetna Open Access -basic- Northern/Central/Southern Maryland Areas	877-459-6604	JN4	JN5	133.79	304.25	61.75	140.42
CareFirst BlueChoice -high- All of Maryland	888-789-9065	2G1	2G2	156.08	360.62	72.04	166.44
CareFirst BlueChoice -std- All of Maryland	888-789-9065	2G4	2G5	135.27	304.32	62.43	140.45
Coventry Health Care -high- All of Maryland	800-833-7423	IG1	IG2	136.99	454.45	63.22	209.75
Coventry Health Care -std- All of Maryland	800-833-7423	IG4	IG5	123.29	312.17	56.90	144.08
Kaiser Foundation Health Plan Mid-Atlantic States -high- Baltimore/Washington, DC areas	877-574-3337	E31	E32	152.81	381.76	70.53	176.20
Kaiser Foundation Health Plan Mid-Atlantic States -std- Baltimore/Washington, DC areas	877-574-3337	E34	E35	94.45	217.24	43.59	100.26
M.D. IPA -high- All of Maryland	877-835-9861	JP1	JP2	166.96	417.79	77.06	192.83

The information contained in this Guide is not the official statement of benefits. Each plan's Federal brochure is the official statement of benefits.

Plan Name – Location	Primary care/ Specialist office copay	Hospital per stay deductible	Prescription Drugs			Member Survey Results						
			Level I	Level II/ Level III	Mail order discount	Overall plan satisfaction	Getting needed care	Getting care quickly	How well doctors communicate	Customer service	Claims processing	Plan Information on Costs
HMO/POS National Average						67.7	85	85.4	93.5	85.2	87.7	66.4
Kentucky												
Aetna Value Plan	$25/$40	20%	$10	30%/50%	Yes							
Humana HP of Ohio-High	$20/$35	$250 x 3 days	$10	$40/$60	Yes							
Humana HP of Ohio-Std	$25/$40	$500 x 3 days	$10	$40/$60	Yes							
Humana Health Plan, Inc. -High	$20/$35	$250/day x 3	$10	$40/$60	Yes	47.2	87.2	79.6	92.9	86.6	86	65.7
Humana Health Plan, Inc. -Std	$25/$40	$500/day x 3	$10	$40/$60	Yes	47.2	87.2	79.6	92.9	86.6	86	65.7
Humana Health Plan, Inc. -High	$20/$35	$250/day x 3	$10	$40/$60	Yes							
Humana Health Plan, Inc. -Std	$25/$40	$500/day x 3	$10	$40/$60	Yes							
Louisiana												
Aetna Value Plan	$25/$40	20%	$10	30%/50%	Yes							
Coventry Health Care of Louisiana-High	$25/$45	Ded+$100	$5	$40/$75	Yes	50	77.7	84	97.5	71.5	84.2	66.9
Coventry Health Care of Louisiana-Std	$30/$55	Ded+30%	$5	$40/$75	Yes	50	77.7	84	97.5	71.5	84.2	66.9
Maine												
Aetna Value Plan	$25/$40	20%	$10	30%/50%	Yes							
Maryland												
Aetna Value Plan	$25/$40	20%	$10	30%/50%	Yes							
Aetna Open Access-High	$15/$30	$150/day x3	$5	$35/$65	Yes	64.9	84.7	85.2	94.3	89.1	85.7	62.1
Aetna Open Access-Basic	$20/$35	10% Plan Allow	$10	$35/$65	Yes	64.9	84.7	85.2	94.3	89.1	85.7	62.1
CareFirst BlueChoice-High	$25/$35	$200	Nothing	$30/$50	Yes	63.1	84.3	87.3	91.5	79.8	85.9	55.8
CareFirst BlueChoice-In-Network	Nothing/$35	$200	Nothing	$30/$50	Yes	63.1	84.3	87.3	91.5	79.8	85.9	55.8
CareFirst BlueChoice-Out-Network	$70/$70	Nothing	Nothing	$30/$50	Yes	63.1	84.3	87.3	91.5	79.8	85.9	55.8
Coventry Health Care-High	$20/$40	$200/day x 3	$3/$15	$30/$60	Yes	55.5	81.8	86.1	92.7	84.3	81.7	54.4
Coventry Health Care-Std	$20/$40	$200/day x 3	$3/$15	$30/$60	Yes	55.5	81.8	86.1	92.7	84.3	81.7	54.4
Kaiser Foundation HP Mid-Atlantic States -High	$10/$20	$100	$7/$17 Net	$30/$50/$45/$65	Yes	55.5	81.8	86.1	92.7	84.3	81.7	54.4
Kaiser Foundation HP Mid-Atlantic States -Std	$20/$30	$250/day x 3	$12/$22Net	$35/$55/$50/$70	Yes	77.8	84.7	85.4	93.2	83.5	75.8	69.6
M.D. IPA-High	$25/$40	$150/day x 3	$7	$30/$60	Yes	57.4	83.5	88.1	92.3	86.1	87.2	67.9

Health Maintenance Organization (HMO) and Point-of-Service (POS) Plans

See page 39 for an explanation of the columns on these pages.

Plan Name – Location	Telephone Number	Enrollment Code		Your Share of Premium			
				Monthly		Biweekly	
		Self only	Self & family	Self only	Self & family	Self only	Self & family
Massachusetts							
Aetna Value Plan - Most of Massachusetts	877-459-6604	EP4	EP5	120.89	274.54	55.80	126.71
Fallon Community Health Plan -basic- Central/Eastern Massachusetts	800-868-5200	JG1	JG2	218.72	615.72	100.95	284.18
Michigan							
Aetna Value Plan-All of Michigan	877-459-6604	G54	G55	122.12	277.32	56.36	127.99
Bluecare Network of MI -high- Traverse City	800-662-6667	H61	H62	123.70	364.88	57.09	168.41
Bluecare Network of MI -high- Grand Rapids	800-662-6667	J31	J32	188.89	644.51	87.18	297.47
Bluecare Network of MI -high- East Region	800-662-6667	K51	K52	201.48	481.17	92.99	222.08
Bluecare Network of MI -high- Southeast Region	800-662-6667	LX1	LX2	166.35	470.27	76.78	217.05
Grand Valley Health Plan -high- Grand Rapids area	616-949-2410	RL1	RL2	239.65	607.62	110.61	280.44
Grand Valley Health Plan -std- Grand Rapids area	616-949-2410	RL4	RL5	196.86	507.52	90.86	234.24
Health Alliance Plan -high- Southeastern Michigan/Flint area	800-556-9765	521	522	175.00	491.59	80.77	226.89
Health Alliance Plan -std- Southeastern Michigan/Flint area	800-556-9765	GY4	GY5	148.20	427.31	68.40	197.22
HealthPlus MI -high- East Michigan	800-332-9161	X51	X52	132.89	460.41	61.33	212.50
Physicians Health Plan -std- Mid-Michigan	866-539-3342	9U4	9U5	120.42	282.00	55.58	130.15
Minnesota							
Aetna Value Plan - Most of Minnesota	877-459-6604	H44	H45	124.69	283.17	57.55	130.69
HealthPartners -High Option - All of Minnesota	800-883-2177	V31	V32	317.83	761.30	146.69	351.37
HealthPartners -Standard Option - All of Minnesota	800-883-2177	V34	V35	89.87	206.71	41.48	95.40
Mississippi							
Aetna Value Plan-Most of Mississippi	877-459-6604	H44	H45	124.69	283.17	57.55	130.69

The information contained in this Guide is not the official statement of benefits. Each plan's Federal brochure is the official statement of benefits.

Plan Name – Location	Primary care/ Specialist office copay	Hospital per stay deductible	Prescription Drugs			Member Survey Results						
			Level I	Level II/ Level III	Mail order discount	Overall plan satisfaction	Getting needed care	Getting care quickly	How well doctors communicate	Customer service	Claims processing	Plan Information on Costs
HMO/POS National Average						67.7	85	85.4	93.5	85.2	87.7	66.4
Massachusetts												
Aetna Value Plan	$25/$40	20%	$10	30%/50%	Yes							
Fallon Community Health Plan-Basic	$25/$35	$150 to $750max	$10	$30/$60	Yes	64	84.1	87.9	94.1	83.5	84.7	61.1
Michigan												
Aetna Value Plan	$25/$40	20%	$10	30%/50%	Yes							
Bluecare Network of MI-High	$10/$15	$200	$10	$30/N/A	Yes	62.2	85.6	87.9	92	87.4	87	60.7
Bluecare Network of MI-High	$10/$15	$200	$10	$30/N/A	Yes	62.2	85.6	87.9	92	87.4	87	60.7
Bluecare Network of MI-High	$15/$25	Nothing	$5	$50/N/A	Yes	62.2	85.6	87.9	92	87.4	87	60.7
Bluecare Network of MI-High	$15/$25	Nothing	$5	$50/N/A	Yes	62.2	85.6	87.9	92	87.4	87	60.7
Grand Valley Health Plan-High	$10/$10	Nothing	$5	$15/$15	No	77	85.4	89.8	92.7	91.1	86.4	78
Grand Valley Health Plan-Std	$20/$20	$500 x 3	$10	$40	No	77	85.4	89.8	92.7	91.1	86.4	78
Health Alliance Plan-High	$10/$20	Nothing	$5	$25/$25	Yes	82.2	86.1	85.8	94	84	91.3	65.3
Health Alliance Plan-Std	$15/$30	Nothing	$10	$40/$40	Yes	82.2	86.1	85.8	94	84	91.3	65.3
HealthPlus MI-High	$10/$20	None	$8	$40/$60	Yes	76.6	85.8	89.7	93.7	90.8	94.2	73.4
Physicians Health Plan-Std	$25/$35	20%	$10	$40/50%	Yes	78	91.2	87.6	93.3	88.4	90.5	71.3
Minnesota												
Aetna Value Plan	$25/$40	20%	$10	30%/50%	Yes							
HealthPartners-High-Option	$25/$45	Nothing	$12	$45/$90	Yes	60.3	85.7	88.2	97.8	90	89.2	68.9
HealthPartners-Std-Option	$0 for 3, then 20%	20% in/40% out	$9	$40/$70	Yes	60.3	85.7	88.2	97.8	90	89.2	68.9
Mississippi												
Aetna Value Plan	$25/$40	20%	$10	30%/50%	Yes							

Health Maintenance Organization (HMO) and Point-of-Service (POS) Plans

See page 39 for an explanation of the columns on these pages.

| Plan Name – Location | Telephone Number | Enrollment Code | | Your Share of Premium | | | |
| | | | | Monthly | | Biweekly | |
		Self only	Self & family	Self only	Self & family	Self only	Self & family
Missouri							
Aetna Value Plan-Most of Missouri	877-459-6604	G54	G55	122.12	277.32	56.36	127.99
Aetna Open Access -high- Kansas City Area	877-459-6604	HY1	HY2	124.05	402.76	57.25	185.89
Blue Preferred Plus POS -high- St. Louis/Central/SW areas	888-811-2092	9G1	9G2	284.29	590.00	131.21	272.31
Coventry Health Care of Kansas -high- Kansas City Metro Area (KS and MO)	800-969-3343	HA1	HA2	129.96	305.41	59.98	140.96
Coventry Health Care of Kansas -std- Kansas City Metro Area (KS and MO)	800-969-3343	HA4	HA5	109.79	258.00	50.67	119.08
Humana Health Plan, Inc. -high- Kansas City	888-393-6765	MS1	MS2	517.61	1150.97	238.90	531.22
Humana Health Plan, Inc. -std- Kansas City	888-393-6765	MS4	MS5	136.81	304.42	63.14	140.50
United Healthcare of the Midwest -high- St. Louis Area	877-835-9861	B91	B92	214.02	481.17	98.78	222.08
Montana							
Aetna Value Plan-South/Southeast/Western MT areas	877-459-6604	H44	H45	124.69	283.17	57.55	130.69
Nebraska							
Aetna Value Plan-All of Nebraska	877-459-6604	H44	H45	124.69	283.17	57.55	130.69
Nevada							
Aetna Value Plan-Las Vegas Area	877-459-6604	G54	G55	122.12	277.32	56.36	127.99
Aetna Open Access -high- Clark County and Las Vegas areas	877-459-6604	HF1	HF2	111.20	375.20	51.32	173.17
Health Plan of Nevada -high- Las Vegas/Esmeralda and Nye counties	877-545-7378	NM1	NM2	98.84	233.06	45.62	107.57
New Hampshire							
Aetna Value Plan-All of New Hampshire	877-459-6604	EP4	EP5	120.89	274.54	55.80	126.71

The information contained in this Guide is not the official statement of benefits. Each plan's federal brochure is the official statement of benefits.

Plan Name – Location	Primary care/ Specialist office copay	Hospital per stay deductible	Prescription Drugs			Member Survey Results						
			Level I	Level II/ Level III	Mail order discount	Overall plan satisfaction	Getting needed care	Getting care quickly	How well doctors communicate	Customer service	Claims processing	Plan Information on Costs
HMO/POS National Average						67.7	85	85.4	93.5	85.2	87.7	66.4
Missouri												
Aetna Value Plan	$25/$40	20%	$10	30%/50%	Yes							
Aetna Open Access-High	$20/$35	$250/day x 4	$10	$35/$65	Yes							
Blue Preferred Plus POS-In-Network	$25/$35	$500	$10	$50/$50/25%/$50/25%	Yes	64.7	89.6	87.5	93.6	82.6	91.1	63.9
Blue Preferred Plus POS-Out-Network	30% after ded.	30% after ded.	N/A	N/A	No	64.7	89.6	87.5	93.6	82.6	91.1	63.9
Coventry Health Care of Kansas-High	$25/$60	25%	$3/$12	$50/$75	Yes	59.1	87.2	87	95.8	86.7	89.2	62.9
Coventry Health Care of Kansas-Std	$30/$60	30%	$3/$12	$50/20%	Yes	59.1	87.2	87	95.8	86.7	89.2	62.9
Humana Health Plan, Inc.-High	$20/$35	$250/day x 3	$10	$40/$60	Yes	66.4	86.3	86.9	93.2	87.2	90.9	72.2
Humana Health Plan, Inc.-Std	$25/$40	$500/day x 3	$10	$40/$60	Yes	66.4	86.3	86.9	93.2	87.2	90.9	72.2
United Healthcare of the Midwest, Inc.-High	$25/$40	$450	$7	$30/$60	Yes	71.4	91.1	89.4	96.7	87.9	92	69.5
Montana												
Aetna Value Plan	$25/$40	20%	$10	30%/50%	Yes							
Nebraska												
Aetna Value Plan	$25/$40	20%	$10	30%/50%	Yes							
Nevada												
Aetna Value Plan	$25/$40	20%	$10	30%/50%	Yes							
Aetna Open Access-High	$20/$35	$250/day x 4	$10	$35/$65	Yes							
Health Plan of Nevada-High	$10/$20	$150	$5	$35/$55	Yes	55.1	73.7	72.7	92.8	83.7	91.3	57.7
New Hampshire												
Aetna Value Plan	$25/$40	20%	$10	30%/50%	Yes							

Health Maintenance Organization (HMO) and Point-of-Service (POS) Plans

See page 39 for an explanation of the columns on these pages.

Plan Name – Location	Telephone Number	Enrollment Code		Your Share of Premium			
				Monthly		Biweekly	
		Self only	Self & family	Self only	Self & family	Self only	Self & family
New Jersey							
Aetna Value Plan-All of New Jersey	877-459-6604	EP4	EP5	120.89	274.54	55.80	126.71
Aetna Open Access -high- Northern New Jersey	877-459-6604	JR1	JR2	507.43	1197.60	234.20	552.74
Aetna Open Access -basic- Northern New Jersey	877-459-6604	JR4	JR5	264.14	643.47	121.91	296.99
Aetna Open Access -high- Southern NJ	877-459-6604	P31	P32	668.00	1688.74	308.31	779.42
Aetna Open Access -basic- Southern NJ	877-459-6604	P34	P35	392.75	940.98	181.27	434.30
GHI Health Plan -high- Northern New Jersey	212-501-4444	801	802	289.38	836.55	133.56	386.10
GHI Health Plan -std- Northern New Jersey	212-501-4444	804	805	128.50	299.97	59.31	138.45
New Mexico							
Aetna Value Plan-Albuquerque/Dona Ana/Hobbs Area	877-459-6604	G54	G55	122.12	277.32	56.36	127.99
Lovelace Health Plan -high- All of New Mexico	800-808-7363	Q11	Q12	119.10	279.88	54.97	129.18
Presbyterian Health Plan -high- All counties in New Mexico	800-356-2219	P21	P22	196.04	463.58	90.48	213.96

The information contained in this Guide is not the official statement of benefits. Each plan's Federal brochure is the official statement of benefits.

Plan Name – Location	Primary care/ Specialist office copay	Hospital per stay deductible	Prescription Drugs			Member Survey Results						
			Level I	Level II/ Level III	Mail order discount	Overall plan satisfaction	Getting needed care	Getting care quickly	How well doctors communicate	Customer service	Claims processing	Plan, Information on Costs
HMO/POS National Average						67.7	85	85.4	93.5	85.2	87.7	66.4
New Jersey												
Aetna Value Plan	$25/$40	20%	$10	30%/50%	Yes							
Aetna Open Access-High	$20/$35	$250/day x 4	$10	$35/$65	Yes	67.1	89.4	89.3	92.2	87.4	83.8	62.8
Aetna Open Access-Basic	$15/$35	20% Plan Allow	$5	$35/$65	Yes	67.1	89.4	89.3	92.2	87.4	83.8	62.8
Aetna Open Access-High	$20/$35	$250/day x 4	$10	$35/$65	Yes	67.1	89.4	89.3	92.2	87.4	83.8	62.8
Aetna Open Access-Basic	$15/$35	20% Plan Allow	$5	$35/$65	Yes	67.1	89.4	89.3	92.2	87.4	83.8	62.8
GHI Health Plan-In-Network	$20/$20	$150max$450	$15	$40/$80	Yes	65.1	91.2	85.3	94.3	85.2	84.2	65.6
GHI Health Plan-Out-Network	+50% of sch.	+50% of sch.	N/A	N/A	No	65.1	91.2	85.3	94.3	85.2	84.2	65.6
GHI Health Plan-Std	$30/$30	$250/day x 3	$5	$40/$80	Yes	65.1	91.2	85.3	94.3	85.2	84.2	65.6
New Mexico												
Aetna Value Plan	$25/$40	20%	$10	30%/50%	Yes							
Lovelace Health Plan-High	$20/$35	$250 after ded	$5	$35/$60/50%	Yes	63.4	80.2	78.2	90.3	77.5	88	73.1
Presbyterian Health Plan-High	$25/$35	$100 x 5 days	$10	$40/$75/30%	Yes	64.2	81.9	80.6	92.2	84.7	88.1	66.6

Health Maintenance Organization (HMO) and Point-of-Service (POS) Plans

See page 39 for an explanation of the columns on these pages.

Plan Name – Location	Telephone Number	Enrollment Code		Your Share of Premium			
				Monthly		Biweekly	
		Self only	Self & family	Self only	Self & family	Self only	Self & family
New York							
Aetna Value Plan-Most of New York	877-459-6604	EP4	EP5	120.89	274.54	55.80	126.71
Aetna Open Access -high- NYC Area/Upstate NY	877-459-6604	JC1	JC2	404.60	1093.04	186.74	504.48
Aetna Open Access -basic- NYC Area/Upstate NY	877-459-6604	JC4	JC5	284.35	774.93	131.24	357.66
Blue Choice -high- Rochester area	800-499-1275	MK1	MK2	292.45	715.78	134.98	330.36
Blue Choice -std- Rochester area	800-499-1275	MK4	MK5	173.89	545.28	80.26	251.67
CDPHP Universal Benefits -high- Upstate, Hudson Valley, Central New York	877-269-2134	SG1	SG2	202.71	649.83	93.56	295.31
CDPHP Universal Benefits -std- Upstate, Hudson Valley, Central New York	877-269-2134	SG4	SG5	115.29	297.44	53.21	137.28
GHI HMO -high- Bronx/Brklyn/Manhat/Queen/Richmon/Westchester	877-244-4466	6V1	6V2	127.26	379.36	58.74	175.09
GHI HMO -high- Capital/Hudson Valley Regions	877-244-4466	X41	X42	153.18	534.56	70.70	246.72
GHI Health Plan -high- All of New York	212-501-4444	801	802	289.38	836.55	133.56	386.10
GHI Health Plan -std- All of New York City	212-501-4444	804	805	128.50	299.97	59.31	138.45
HIP Health of Greater New York -High- New York City area including Long Island	1-800-447-8255	511	512	224.42	769.77	103.58	355.28
HIP Health of Greater New York -Std- New York City area including Long Island	1-800-447-8255	514	515	156.17	588.87	72.08	271.79
Independent Health Assoc -high- Western New York	800-501-3439	QA1	QA2	192.83	595.09	89.00	274.66
Independent Health Association -Std- Western New York	800-501-8439	C54	C55	174.72	549.77	80.64	253.74
MVP Health Care -high- Eastern Region	888-687-6277	GA1	GA2	146.16	480.19	67.46	221.63
MVP Health Care -std- Eastern Region	888-687-6277	GA4	GA5	127.84	349.00	59.00	161.08
MVP Health Care -high- Western Region	888-687-6277	GV1	GV2	119.62	299.32	55.21	138.15
MVP Health Care -std- Western Region	888-687-6277	GV4	GV5	106.75	267.09	49.27	123.27
MVP Health Care -high- Central Region	888-687-6277	M91	M92	183.02	574.47	84.47	265.14
MVP Health Care -std- Central Region	888-687-6277	M94	M95	135.53	435.32	62.55	200.92
MVP Health Care -high- Northern Region	888-687-6277	MF1	MF2	229.79	664.69	106.06	306.78
MVP Health Care -std- Northern Region	888-687-6277	MF4	MF5	129.16	372.06	59.61	171.72
MVP Health Care -high- Mid-Hudson Region	888-687-6277	MX1	MX2	171.84	544.28	79.31	251.21
MVP Health Care -std- Mid-Hudson Region	888-687-6277	MX4	MX5	132.25	408.09	61.04	188.35
North Carolina							
Aetna Value Plan-All of North Carolina	877-459-6604	F54	F55	124.37	282.43	57.40	130.35

The information contained in this Guide is not the official statement of benefits. Each plan's Federal brochure is the official statement of benefits.

Plan Name – Location	Primary care/ Specialist office copay	Hospital per stay deductible	Prescription Drugs			Member Survey Results						
			Level I	Level II/ Level III	Mail order discount	Overall plan satisfaction	Getting needed care	Getting care quickly	How well doctors communicate	Customer service	Claims processing	Plan Information on Costs
HMO/POS National Average						67.7	85	85.4	93.5	85.2	87.7	66.4

New York

Plan Name – Location	Primary care/ Specialist office copay	Hospital per stay deductible	Level I	Level II/ Level III	Mail order discount	Overall plan satisfaction	Getting needed care	Getting care quickly	How well doctors communicate	Customer service	Claims processing	Plan Information on Costs
Aetna Value Plan	$25/$40	20%	$10	30%/50%	Yes							
Aetna Open Access-High	$20/$35	$250/day x 4	$10	$35/$65	Yes	67	86	85.4	95.2	84.8	86.1	55.6
Aetna Open Access-Basic	$15/$35	20% Plan Allow	$5	$35/$65	Yes	67	86	85.4	95.2	84.8	86.1	55.6
Blue Choice-High	$20/$20	$240	$10	$30/$50	No	70.6	85.6	87.1	93.9	84.1	88	67
Blue Choice-Std	$25/$40	$500	$7	$50/$100	No	70.6	85.6	87.1	93.9	84.1	88	67
CDPHP Universal Benefits, Inc.-High	$20/$30	$100 x 5	25%	25%/25%	No	72.9	89.6	90.9	96.2	90.6	91.1	74.3
CDPHP Universal Benefits, Inc.-Std	$25/$40	$500+10%	30%	30%/30%	No	72.9	89.6	90.9	96.2	90.6	91.1	74.3
GHI HMO Select-High	$25/$40	$500	$10	$30/$50	Yes							
GHI HMO Select-High	$25/$40	$500	$10	$30/$50	Yes							
GHI Health Plan-In-Network	$20/$20	$150max$450	$15	$40/$80	Yes	65.1	91.2	85.3	94.3	85.2	84.2	65.6
GHI Health Plan-Out-Network	+50% of sch	+50% of sch.	N/A	N/A	No	65.1	91.2	85.3	94.3	85.2	84.2	65.6
GHI Health Plan-Std	$30/$30	$250/day x 3	$5	$40/$80	Yes	65.1	91.2	85.3	94.3	85.2	84.2	65.6
HIP of Greater New York-High	$20/$40	None	$30/$100Ded	$30/$50/	Yes	73.8	79.8	79.6	91.8	85.3	89.8	55.5
HIP of Greater New York Std	$20/$50	$500	$20 after Ded	$30/$50/$100Ded	Yes	73.8	79.8	79.6	91.8	85.3	89.8	55.5
Independent Health Assoc.-In-Network	$20/$20	$250	$10	$20/$35	No	75.4	87.6	89.1	92.4	89.1	90.2	76.6
Independent Health Assoc.-Out-Network	25%/25%	25%	N/A	N/A	No	75.4	87.6	89.1	92.4	89.1	90.2	76.6
Independent Health Association-In-Network	$25/$40	$500	$10	$30/$75	Yes							
Independent Health Association-Out-Network	30%/30%	30%	N/A	N/A	No							
MVP Health Care-High	$25/$25	$500	$5	$35/$70	Yes	68.3	90.1	93.1	95.8	91.6	88.9	79.5
MVP Health Care-Std	$30/$50	$750	$5	$45/$90	Yes	68.3	90.1	93.1	95.8	91.6	88.9	79.5
MVP Health Care-High	$25/$25	$500	$5	$35/$70	Yes	68.3	90.1	93.1	95.8	91.6	88.9	79.5
MVP Health Care-Std	$30/$50	$750	$5	$45/$90	Yes	68.3	90.1	93.1	95.8	91.6	88.9	79.5
MVP Health Care-High	$25/$25	$500	$5	$35/$70	Yes	68.3	90.1	93.1	95.8	91.6	88.9	79.5
MVP Health Care-Std	$30/$50	$750	$5	$45/$90	Yes	68.3	90.1	93.1	95.8	91.6	88.9	79.5
MVP Health Care-High	$25/$25	$500	$5	$35/$70	Yes	68.3	90.1	93.1	95.8	91.6	88.9	79.5
MVP Health Care-Std	$30/$50	$750	$5	$45/$90	Yes	68.3	90.1	93.1	95.8	91.6	88.9	79.5

North Carolina

Plan Name – Location	Primary care/ Specialist office copay	Hospital per stay deductible	Level I	Level II/ Level III	Mail order discount	Overall plan satisfaction	Getting needed care	Getting care quickly	How well doctors communicate	Customer service	Claims processing	Plan Information on Costs
Aetna Value Plan	$25/$40	20%	$10	30%/50%	Yes							

Health Maintenance Organization (HMO) and Point-of-Service (POS) Plans

See page 39 for an explanation of the columns on these pages.

| Plan Name – Location | Telephone Number | Enrollment Code | | Your Share of Premium | | | |
| | | | | Monthly | | Biweekly | |
		Self only	Self & family	Self only	Self & family	Self only	Self & family
North Dakota							
Aetna Value Plan-Most of North Dakota	877-459-6604	H44	H45	124.69	283.17	57.55	130.69
HealthPartners -High Option-Eastern North Dakota	800-883-2177	V31	V32	317.83	761.30	146.69	351.37
HealthPartners -Standard Option-Eastern North Dakota	800-883-2177	V34	V35	89.87	206.71	41.48	95.40
Heart of America Health Plan -high- Northcentral North Dakota	800-525-5661	RU1	RU2	123.48	348.70	56.99	160.94
Sanford Health Plan-High-North Dakota	800-752-5863	C91	C92	222.41	541.86	102.65	250.09
Sanford Health Plan-Std-North Dakota	800-752-5863	C94	C95	152.25	485.81	70.27	224.22
Ohio							
AultCare HMO -High- Stark/Carroll/Holmes/Tuscarawas/Wayne Co.	330-363-6360	3A1	3A2	135.24	407.44	62.42	188.05
Humana Health Plan of Ohio-High Greater Cincinnati Area	888-393-6765	A61	A62	129.99	289.24	60.00	133.49
Humana Health Plan of Ohio-Standard Greater Cincinnati Area	888-393-6765	A64	A65	116.99	260.31	54.00	120.14
Kaiser Foundation Health Plan of Ohio -High- Cleveland/Akron areas	800-686-7100	641	642	258.37	624.52	119.25	288.24
Kaiser Foundation Health Plan of Ohio -Standard- Cleveland/Akron areas	800-686-7100	644	645	115.76	266.27	53.43	122.89
The Health Plan of the Upper Ohio Valley -High-Eastern Ohio	800-624-6961	U41	U42	250.98	580.97	115.84	268.14
Oklahoma							
Globalhealth, Inc. -high- Oklahoma	877-280-5600	IM1	IM2	105.72	254.77	48.79	117.59
Oregon							
Aetna Value Plan-Most of Oregon	877-459-6604	H44	H45	124.69	283.17	57.55	130.69
Kaiser Foundation Health Plan of Northwest -High- Portland/Salem areas	800-813-2000	571	572	212.40	492.91	98.03	227.50
Kaiser Foundation Health Plan of Northwest -Std- Portland/Salem areas	800-813-2000	574	575	126.21	289.95	58.25	133.82
Kaiser Foundation Health Plan of Northwest -Basic- Portland/Salem areas	800-813-2000	B51	B52	116.01	266.50	53.54	123.00

The information contained in this Guide is not the official statement of benefits. Each plan's Federal brochure is the official statement of benefits.

Plan Name – Location	Primary care/ Specialist office copay	Hospital per stay deductible	Prescription Drugs		Mail order discount	Member Survey Results						
			Level I	Level II/ Level III		Overall plan satisfaction	Getting needed care	Getting care quickly	How well doctors communicate	Customer service	Claims processing	Plan Information on Costs
HMO/POS National Average						67.7	85	85.4	93.5	85.2	87.7	66.4
North Dakota												
Aetna Value Plan	$25/$40	20%	$10	30%/50%	Yes							
HealthPartners-High-Option	$25/$45	Nothing	$12	$45/$90	Yes	60.3	85.7	88.2	97.8	90	89.2	68.9
HealthPartners-Std-Option	$0 for 3, then 20%	20% in/40% out	$9	$40/$70	Yes	60.3	85.7	88.2	97.8	90	89.2	68.9
Heart of America Health Plan-High-In-Network	$15/$25	None	50%/$600ded	50%/$600ded/50%/$600ded	No							
Heart of America Health Plan-High-Out-Network	20%/20%	20%	N/A	N/A	No							
Sanford HP-In-Network-High	$20/$30	$100/day x 5	$15	$30/$50	NO							
Sanford HP-Out-Network-High	40%/40%	40%	40%+	40%+	No							
Sanford HP-In-Network-Std	$25/$25	$100/day x 5	$15	$30/$50	No							
Sanford HP-Out-Network-Std	40%/40%	40%	40%+	40%+	No							
Ohio												
AultCare HMO-High	$15/$20	$150	$15	$30/$45	No	89.7	92.6	93	96	94.8	94.7	85.7
Humana HP of Ohio-High	$20/$35	$250 x 3 days	$10	$40/$60	Yes							
Humana HP of Ohio-Standard	$25/$45	$500 x 3 days	$10	$40/$60	Yes							
Kaiser Foundation HP of Ohio-High	$20/$20	$250	$10	$30/$30	Yes	76.5	82.7	86.9	92.9	83.3	87.1	71.8
Kaiser Foundation HP of Ohio-Std	$30/$40	$500	$15	$40/$40	Yes	76.5	82.7	86.9	92.9	83.3	87.1	71.8
The Health Plan of the Upper Ohio Valley-High	$10/$20	$250	$15	$30/$50	Yes	75.4	91.6	86.3	93.3	90.7	94.7	75.5
Oklahoma												
Globalhealth, Inc.-High	$15/$45	$250 day max $1000	$4/$10	$45/$65	Yes	62	77.2	85	92.5	85.8	88	70.7
Oregon												
Aetna Value Plan	$25/$40	20%	$10	30%/50%	Yes							
Kaiser Foundation HP of Northwest-High	$20/$30	$200	$15	$40/$60	Yes	71.8	80.4	81	91.6	83.5	78	65.8
Kaiser Foundation HP of Northwest-Std	$25/$35	$500	$20	$40/$60	Yes	71.8	80.4	81	91.6	83.5	78	65.8
Kaiser Foundation HP of Northwest-Basic	$35/$45	$500	$20	$40/$60	Yes							

Health Maintenance Organization (HMO) and Point-of-Service (POS) Plans

See page 39 for an explanation of the columns on these pages.

Plan Name – Location	Telephone Number	Enrollment Code		Your Share of Premium			
				Monthly		Biweekly	
		Self only	Self & family	Self only	Self & family	Self only	Self & family
Pennsylvania							
Aetna Value Plan-All of Pennsylvania	877-459-6604	H44	H45	124.69	283.17	57.55	130.69
Aetna Open Access -High- Philadelphia	877-459-6604	P31	P32	668.00	1688.74	308.31	779.42
Aetna Open Access -Basic- Philadelphia	877-459-6604	P34	P35	392.75	940.98	181.27	434.30
Aetna Open Access -High- Pittsburgh and Western PA Areas	877-459-6604	YE1	YE2	129.72	377.19	59.87	174.09
Geisinger Health Plan -Std- Northeastern/Central/South Central areas	800-447-4000	GG4	GG5	231.09	561.86	106.66	259.32
HealthAmerica Pennsylvania -High- Greater Pittsburgh area	866-351-5946	261	262	183.30	481.73	84.60	222.34
UPMC Health Plan -High- Western Pennsylvania	877-648-9641	8W1	8W2	218.12	531.96	100.67	245.52
UPMC Health Plan -Std- Western Pennsylvania	877-648-9641	UW4	UW5	133.14	306.22	61.45	141.33
Puerto Rico							
Humana Health Plans of Puerto Rico, Inc. -high- Puerto Rico	800-314-3121	ZJ1	ZJ2	82.33	183.17	38.00	84.54
Triple-S Salud, Inc. -high- All of Puerto Rico	787-774-6060	891	892	83.89	188.75	38.72	87.12
Rhode Island							
Aetna Value Plan-All of Rhode Island	877-459-6604	EP4	EP5	120.89	274.54	55.80	126.71
South Dakota							
Aetna Value Plan-Rapid City/Sioux Falls Area	877-459-6604	G54	G55	122.12	277.32	56.36	127.99
HealthPartners -High Option-Eastern South Dakota	800-883-2177	V31	V32	317.83	761.30	146.69	351.37
HealthPartners -Standard Option-Eastern South Dakota	800-883-2177	V34	V35	89.87	206.71	41.48	95.40
Sanford Health Plan -High- Eastern/Central/Rapid City Areas	800-752-5863	AU1	AU2	243.18	590.13	112.24	272.37
Sanford Health Plan -std- Eastern/Central/Rapid City Areas	800-752-5863	AU4	AU5	218.03	531.80	100.63	245.45

The information contained in this Guide is not the official statement of benefits. Each plan's Federal brochure is the official statement of benefits.

Plan Name – Location	Primary care/ Specialist office copay	Hospital per stay deductible	Prescription Drugs			Member Survey Results						
			Level I	Level II/ Level III	Mail order discount	Overall plan satisfaction	Getting needed care	Getting care quickly	How well doctors communicate	Customer service	Claims processing	Plan Information on Costs
HMO/POS National Average						67.7	85	85.4	93.5	85.2	87.7	66.4
Pennsylvania												
Aetna Value Plan	$25/$40	20%	$10	30%/50%	Yes							
Aetna Open Access-High	$20/$35	$250/day x 4	$10	$35/$65	Yes	53.7	84.2	89.9	94	85.1	89	65.8
Aetna Open Access-Basic	$15/$35	20% Plan Allow	$5	$35/$65	Yes	53.7	84.2	89.9	94	85.1	89	65.8
Aetna Open Access-High	$20/$35	$250/day x 4	$10	$35/$65	Yes	53.7	84.2	89.9	94	85.1	89	65.8
Geisinger Health Plan-Std	$20/$35	20%aftrDeduct	30% $5/$15	40% $40/$120/ 50% $60/$180	Yes	68.4	85	87.7	95.6	86.7	94.7	68.4
HealthAmerica Pennsylvania-High	$25/$50	15%	$5	$35/$60	Yes	71.2	89.7	93.2	95.4	87.2	89.6	68.6
UPMC Health Plan-High	10% after Ded	10% after Ded	$5	$35 after Ded/ $70 after Ded	Yes	79.4	87.8	88.2	95.2	86	89.9	69.7
UPMC Health Plan-Std	20% after Ded	20% after Ded	$5	$35/$70	Yes	79.4	87.8	88.2	95.2	86	89.9	69.7
Puerto Rico												
Humana HP of Puerto Rico -In-Network	$5/$5	None	$2.50	$10/$15	Yes	79.3	80.5	82.2	96.7	79.1	78.7	58.4
Humana HP of Puerto Rico -Out-Network	$10/$10	$50	N/A	N/A	No	79.3	80.5	82.2	96.7	79.1	78.7	58.4
Triple-S Salud, Inc.-In-Network	$7.50/$10	None	$5 or $12	Greater of $5 or 20%/ 20% up to $100/$75 max	Yes	75.7	86.1	84.2	96.7	77.7	78.3	56
Triple-S Salud, Inc.-Out-Network	$7.50+10%/$10+10%	10% +	N/A	N/A	No	75.7	86.1	84.2	96.7	77.7	78.3	56
Rhode Island												
Aetna Value Plan	$25/$40	20%	$10	30%/50%	Yes							
South Dakota												
Aetna Value Plan	$25/$40	20%	$10	30%/50%	Yes							
HealthPartners-High-Option	$25/$45	Nothing	$12	$45/$90	Yes	60.3	85.7	88.2	97.8	90	89.2	68.9
HealthPartners-Std-Option	$0 for 3, then 20%	20% In/40% out	$9	$40/$70	Yes	60.3	85.7	88.2	97.8	90	89.2	68.9
Sanford Health Plan-In-Network-High	$20/$30	$100/day x 5	$15	$30/$50	No	52.3	83.9	86.6	96	83.1	91	65.6
Sanford Health Plan-Out-Network-High	40%/40%	40%	40%+	40%+	No	52.3	83.	86.6	96	83.1	91	65.6
Sanford Health Plan-In-Network-Std	$25/$25	$100/day x 5	$15	$30/$50	No	52.3	83.9	86.6	96	83.1	91	65.6
Sanford Health Plan-Out-Network-Std	40%/40%	40%	40%+	40%+	No	52.3	83.9	86.6	96	83.1	91	65.6

Health Maintenance Organization (HMO) and Point-of-Service (POS) Plans

See page 39 for an explanation of the columns on these pages.

Plan Name – Location	Telephone Number	Enrollment Code		Your Share of Premium			
				Monthly		Biweekly	
		Self only	Self & family	Self only	Self & family	Self only	Self & family
Tennessee							
Aetna Value Plan-Most of Tennessee	877-459-6604	F54	F55	124.37	282.43	57.40	130.35
Aetna Open Access -high- Memphis Area	877-459-6604	UB1	UB2	253.37	779.61	116.94	359.82
Humana Health Plan, Inc. -High- Knoxville	888-393-6765	GJ1	GJ2	136.84	304.46	63.16	140.52
Humana Health Plan, Inc. -Std- Knoxville	888-393-6765	GJ4	GJ5	116.99	260.31	54.00	120.14
Texas							
Aetna Open Access -High- Austin and San Antonio Areas	877-459-6604	P11	P12	382.39	1084.26	176.49	500.43
Aetna Whole Health-Basic-Ft Bend, Harris, Montgomery counties	877-459-6604	ES1	ES2	120.92	354.27	55.81	163.51
Firstcare-High - Central Waco area	800-884-4901	B71	B72	98.38	295.14	45.40	136.22
Firstcare -high- West Texas	800-884-4901	CK1	CK2	100.09	300.27	46.19	138.58
Firstcare-High-Taylor/Callahan/Eastland	800-884-4901	CN1	CN2	119.14	509.01	54.99	234.93
Firstcare-High-Lubbock area	800-884-4901	CZ1	CZ2	115.94	470.60	53.51	217.20
Firstcare-High-Robertson/Brazos/Grimes/Madison/WA	800-884-4901	ET1	ET2	112.43	428.50	51.89	197.77
Humana Health Plan of Texas -High- Corpus Christi	888-393-6765	UC1	UC2	225.85	501.77	104.24	231.59
Humana Health Plan of Texas -Std- Corpus Christi	888-393-6765	UC4	UC5	136.84	304.46	63.16	140.52
Humana Health Plan of Texas -High- San Antonio	888-393-6765	UR1	UR2	481.06	1069.64	222.03	493.68
Humana Health Plan of Texas -Std- San Antonio	888-393-6765	UR4	UR5	136.83	304.46	63.15	140.52
Humana Health Plan of Texas -High- Austin	888-393-6765	UU1	UU2	216.62	481.21	99.98	222.10
Humana Health Plan of Texas -Std- Austin	888-393-6765	UU4	UU5	136.84	304.46	63.16	140.52
UnitedHealthcare Benefits of Texas, Inc. -High- San Antonio	866-546-0510	GF1	GF2	206.65	506.13	95.38	233.60
Utah							
Aetna Value Plan-Most of Utah	877-459-6604	G54	G55	122.12	277.32	56.36	127.99
Altius Health Plans -High- Wasatch Front	800-377-4161	9K1	9K2	210.84	452.87	97.31	209.02
Altius Health Plans -Std- Wasatch Front	800-377-4161	DK4	DK5	112.90	248.37	52.11	114.63
SelectHealth -High- Urban and Suburban Utah	800-538-5038	SF1	SF2	204.75	458.40	94.50	211.57
SelectHealth -Basic- Urban and Suburban Utah	800-538-5038	SF4	SF5	139.21	312.19	64.25	144.09

The information contained in this Guide is not the official statement of benefits. Each plan's Federal brochure is the official statement of benefits.

Plan Name – Location	Primary care/Specialist office copay	Hospital per stay deductible	Prescription Drugs			Member Survey Results						
			Level I	Level II/Level III	Mail order discount	Overall plan satisfaction	Getting needed care	Getting care quickly	How well doctors communicate	Customer service	Claims processing	Plan Information on Costs
HMO/POS National Average						67.7	85	85.4	93.5	85.2	87.7	66.4
Tennessee												
Aetna Value Plan	$25/$40	20%	$10	30%/50%	Yes							
Aetna Open Access-High	$20/$35	$250/day x 4	$10	$35/$65	Yes	72.5	85.2	84.4	90.4	87.6	92.6	70.2
Humana Health Plan, Inc.-High	$20/$35	$250/day x 3	$10	$40/$60	Yes							
Humana Health Plan, Inc.-Std	$25/$40	$500/day x 3	$10	$40/$60	Yes							
Texas												
Aetna Open Access-High	$20/$35	$250/day x 4	$10	$35/$65	Yes	62.8	87	86.9	90.3	82.2	88.9	62.7
Aetna Whole Health-In-Network	$25/$35	15%	$5	$35/$60	Yes							
Aetna Whole Health-Out-Network	50%/50%	50%	40%	40%/40%	No							
Firstcare-High	$30/$55	$250/day x 5	$10	$35/$70	No							
Firstcare-High	$30/$55	$250/day x 5	$10	$35/$70	No							
Firstcare-High	$30/$55	$250/day x 5	$10	$35/$70	No							
Firstcare-High	$30/$55	$250/day x 5	$10	$35/$70	No							
Firstcare-High	$30/$55	$250/day x 5	$10	$35/$70	No							
Humana Health Plan of Texas-High	$20/$35	$250/day x 3	$10	$40/$60	Yes							
Humana Health Plan of Texas-Std	$25/$40	$500/day x 3	$10	$40/$60	Yes							
Humana Health Plan of Texas-High	$20/$35	$250/day x 3	$10	$40/$60	Yes	68.9	86	84.6	92.5	79.1	91.8	64.4
Humana Health Plan of Texas-Std	$25/$40	$500/day x 3	$10	$40/$60	Yes	68.9	86	84.6	92.5	79.1	91.8	64.4
Humana Health Plan of Texas-High	$20/$35	$250/day x 3	$10	$40/$60	Yes	57.8	84.7	85.7	92.6	87	89.6	65.9
Humana Health Plan of Texas-Std	$25/$40	$500/day x 3	$10	$40/$60	Yes	57.8	84.7	85.7	92.6	87	89.6	65.9
UnitedHealthcare Benefits of Texas,Inc.-High	$20/$40	$250/day x 5	$10	$35/$60	Yes	66.7	81.7	85.5	93.4	80.9	89.3	56.9
Utah												
Aetna Value Plan	$25/$40	20%	$10	30%/50%	Yes							
Altius Health Plans-High	$20/$30	$200	$7	$25/$50	Yes	60.8	86.5	89.6	94.7	82.1	88.3	60.7
Altius Health Plans-Standard	$20/$35	None	$7	$35/$60	Yes	60.8	86.5	89.6	94.7	82.1	88.3	60.7
SelectHealth-High	$15/$25	$100	$5/$25/$50	$25,$50/$50	Yes	62.7	85.2	84.5	94.2	92.3	92.4	67
SelectHealth-Standard	$20/$30	$100 after	$5/$25/$50	$25,$50/$50	Yes							

Health Maintenance Organization (HMO) and Point-of-Service (POS) Plans

See page 39 for an explanation of the columns on these pages.

| Plan Name – Location | Telephone Number | Enrollment Code | | Your Share of Premium | | | |
| | | | | Monthly | | Biweekly | |
		Self only	Self & family	Self only	Self & family	Self only	Self & family
Vermont							
Aetna Value Plan-All of Vermont	877-459-6604	EP4	EP5	120.89	274.54	55.80	126.71
Virgin Islands							
Triple-S Salud, Inc. -high- US Virgin Islands	800-981-3241	851	852	103.05	234.02	47.56	108.01
Virginia							
Aetna Value Plan-Most of Virginia	877-459-6604	F54	F55	124.37	282.43	57.40	130.35
Aetna Open Access -high- Northern/Central/Richmond Virginia Areas	877-459-6604	JN1	JN2	436.06	982.17	201.26	453.31
Aetna Open Access -basic- Northern/Central/Richmond Virginia Areas	877-459-6604	JN4	JN5	133.79	304.25	61.75	140.42
Aetna Whole Health-Basic-Various counties in Southwest Virginia	877-459-6604	D91	D92	114.51	354.27	52.85	163.51
CareFirst BlueChoice-High- Northern Virginia	888-789-9065	2G1	2G2	156.08	360.62	72.04	166.44
CareFirst BlueChoice-Std- Northern Virginia	888-789-9065	2G4	2G5	135.27	304.32	62.43	140.45
Kaiser Foundation Health Plan Mid-Atlantic States -high- Northern Virginia/Fredericksburg area	877-574-3337	E31	E32	152.81	381.76	70.53	176.20
Kaiser Foundation Health Plan Mid-Atlantic States -std- Northern Virginia/Fredericksburg area	877-574-3337	E34	R35	94.45	217.24	43.59	100.26
M.D. IPA -High- Northern Virginia	877-835-9861	JP1	JP2	166.96	417.79	77.06	192.83
Optima Health Plan -high- Hampton Roads and Richmond areas	800-206-1060	9R1	9R2	201.30	533.97	92.91	246.45
Optima Health Plan -std- Hampton Roads and Richmond areas	800-206-1060	9R4	9R5	97.99	231.87	45.23	107.02
Piedmont Community Healthcare -high- Lynchburg area	888-674-3368	2C1	2C2	128.80	294.93	59.44	136.12

The information contained in this Guide is not the official statement of benefits. Each plan's Federal brochure is the official statement of benefits.

Plan Name – Location	Primary care/ Specialist office copay	Hospital per stay deductible	Prescription Drugs			Member Survey Results						
			Level I	Level II/ Level III	Mail order discount	Overall plan satisfaction	Getting needed care	Getting care quickly	How well doctors communicate	Customer service	Claims processing	Plan Information on Costs
HMO/POS National Average						67.7	85	85.4	93.5	85.2	87.7	66.4
Vermont												
Aetna Value Plan	$25/$40	20%	$10	30%/50%	Yes							
Virgin Islands												
Triple-S Salud, Inc.-In-Network	$7.50/$10	None	$5 or $12	Greater of $15 or 20%/ 20% up to $100/$175 coin	Yes	75.7	86.1	84.2	96.7	77.7	78.3	56
Triple-S Salud, Inc.-Out-Network	$7.50 & 10%+/ $10 & 10%+	10%+	N/A	N/A	No	75.7	86.1	84.2	96.7	77.7	78.3	56
Virginia												
Aetna Value Plan	$25/$40	20%	$10	30%/50%	Yes							
Aetna Open Access-High	$15/$30	$150/day x3	$5	$35/$65	Yes	64.9	84.7	85.2	94.3	89.1	85.7	62.1
Aetna Open Access-Basic	$20/$35	10% Plan Allow	$10	$35/$65	Yes	64.9	84.7	85.2	94.3	89.1	85.7	62.1
Aetna Whole Health-In-Network	$25/$35	15%	$5	$35/$60	Yes							
Aetna Whole Health-Out-Network	40%/40%	40%	40%	40%/40%	No							
CareFirst BlueChoice-High	$25/$35	$200	Nothing	$30/$50	Yes	63.1	84.3	87.3	91.5	79.8	85.9	55.8
CareFirst BlueChoice-In-Network	Nothing/$35	$200	Nothing	$30/$50	Yes	63.1	84.3	87.3	91.5	79.8	85.9	55.8
CareFirst BlueChoice-Out-Network	$70/$70	$500	Nothing	$30/$50	Yes	63.1	84.3	87.3	91.5	79.8	85.9	55.8
Kaiser Foundation HP Mid-Atlantic-High	$10/$20	$100	$7/$17 Net	$30/$30/$6/$65	Yes	77.8	84.7	85.4	93.2	83.5	75.8	69.6
Kaiser Foundation HP-Mid-Atlantic-Std	$20/$30	$250/day x 3	$12/$22 Net	$35/$55/$50/$70	Yes	77.8	84.7	85.4	93.2	83.5	75.8	69.6
M.D. IPA-High	$25/$40	$150/day x 3	$7	$30/$60	Yes	57.4	83.5	88.1	92.5	86.1	87.2	67.9
Optima Health Plan-High	$15/$40 child <22/$30	$150 max $750	$10	$30/50%-50% up to $5,000	Yes	70.9	89.5	89.1	95.6	89.9	93.8	73.6
Optima Health Plan-Std	$20/$30	None	$10	$30/50%-50% up to $5,000	No	70.9	89.5	89.1	95.6	89.9	93.8	73.6
Piedmont Community HC-High	$35/$35	20%	$15	$40/$55	Yes							

Health Maintenance Organization (HMO) and Point-of-Service (POS) Plans

See page 39 for an explanation of the columns on these pages.

| Plan Name – Location | Telephone Number | Enrollment Code | | Your Share of Premium | | | |
| | | | | Monthly | | Biweekly | |
		Self only	Self & family	Self only	Self & family	Self only	Self & family
Washington							
Aetna Value Plan -Most of Washington	877-459-6604	G54	G55	122.12	277.32	56.36	127.99
Aetna Open Access -High- Seattle & Spokane	877-459-6604	C31	C32	135.72	561.27	62.64	259.05
Group Health Cooperative -High- Western WA/Central WA/Spokane/Pullman	888-901-4636	541	542	242.01	488.64	111.70	225.53
Group Health Cooperative -Std- Western WA/Central WA/Spokane/Pullman	888-901-4636	544	545	105.37	237.90	48.63	109.80
KPS Health Plans -Std- All of Washington	800-552-7114	L11	L12	111.01	239.62	51.23	110.59
KPS Health Plans -High- All of Washington	800-552-7114	VT1	VT2	272.35	577.89	125.70	266.72
Kaiser Foundation Health Plan of Northwest -High- Vancouver/Longview	800-813-2000	571	572	212.40	492.91	98.03	227.50
Kaiser Foundation Health Plan of Northwest -Std- Vancouver/Longview	800-813-2000	574	575	126.21	289.95	58.25	133.82
Kaiser Foundation Health Plan of the Northwest -Basic- Vancouver/Longview	800-813-2000	B51	B52	116.01	266.50	53.54	123.00
West Virginia							
Aetna Value Plan-Most of West Virginia	877-459-6604	F54	F55	124.37	282.43	57.40	130.35
The Health Plan of the Upper Ohio Valley -high- Northern/Central West Virginia	800-624-6961	U41	U42	250.98	580.97	115.84	268.14
Wisconsin							
Aetna Whole Health-Basic Various Counties in Southeastern WI	877-459-6604	F71	F72	100.00	275.55	46.15	127.18
Dean Health Plan -high- South Central Wisconsin	800-279-1301	WD1	WD2	209.43	636.52	96.66	293.78
Group Health Cooperative -high- South Central Wisconsin	800-650-4327	WJ1	WJ2	130.89	388.63	60.41	179.37
HealthPartners -High Option-Western Wisconsin	800-883-2177	V31	V32	317.83	761.30	146.69	351.37
HealthPartners -Standard Option-Western Wisconsin	800-883-2177	V34	V35	89.87	206.71	41.48	95.40
MercyCare HMO -High- South Central Wisconsin	800-895-2421	EY1	EY2	130.15	381.37	60.07	176.02
Physicians Plus -High- Dane County	800-545-5015	LW1	LW2	127.21	376.95	58.71	173.98
Wyoming							
Aetna Value Plan-All of Wyoming	877-459-6604	H44	H45	124.69	283.17	57.55	130.69
Altius Health Plans -high- Uinta County	800-377-4161	9K1	9K2	210.84	452.87	97.31	209.02
Altius Health Plans -std- Uinta County	800-377-4161	DK4	DK5	112.90	248.37	52.11	114.63

The information contained in this Guide is not the official statement of benefits. Each plan's Federal brochure is the official statement of benefits.

Plan Name – Location	Primary care/ Specialist office copay	Hospital per stay deductible	Prescription Drugs Level I	Level II/ Level III	Mail order discount	Overall plan satisfaction	Getting needed care	Getting care quickly	How well doctors communicate	Customer service	Claims processing	Plan Information on Costs
				HMO/POS National Average		67.7	85	85.4	93.5	85.2	87.7	66.4
Washington												
Aetna Value Plan	$25/$40	20%	$10	30%/50%	Yes							
Aetna Open Access-High	$20/$35	$250/day x 4	$10	$35/$65	Yes							
Group Health Cooperative-High	$25/$25	$350/day x 3	$20	$40/$60	Yes	70.9	82.8	86.2	92.1	85.5	91.5	71.3
Group Health Cooperative-Standard	4/$25-$25+20%	$500/day x 3	$20	$40/$60	Yes	70.9	82.8	86.2	92.1	85.5	91.5	71.3
KPS Health Plans-In-Network	$15/3 or 20%/20%	Nothing	$10	$35/50%/ $40max$100	Yes	77.3	92.1	92.1	95.6	91.7	94.7	68.2
KPS Health Plans-Out-Network	$15/3 +40%+diff/ 40%+diff	Nothing	Not Covered	Not Covered	No	77.3	92.1	92.1	95.6	91.7	94.7	68.2
KPS Health Plans-In-Network	$30/$30	None	$5	$25/50% or $100	Yes	77.3	92.1	92.1	95.6	91.7	94.7	68.2
KPS Health Plans-Out-Network	$30+40%+diff	None	Not covered	N/A	No	77.3	92.1	92.1	95.6	91.7	94.7	68.2
Kaiser Foundation HP of Northwest-High	$20/$30	$200	$15	$40/$60	Yes	71.8	80.4	81	91.6	83.5	78	65.8
Kaiser Foundation HP of Northwest-Standard	$25/$35	$500	$20	$40/$60	Yes	71.8	80.4	81	91.6	83.5	78	65.8
Kaiser Foundation HP of the NW-Basic	$35/$45	$500	$20	$40/$60	Yes							
West Virginia												
Aetna Value Plan	$25/$40	20%	$10	50%/50%	Yes							
The HP of the Upper Ohio Valley-High	$10/$20	$250	$15	$30/$50	Yes	75.4	91.6	86.3	93.3	90.7	94.7	75.5
Wisconsin												
Aetna Whole Health-In-Network	$25/$35	15%	$5	$35/$60	Yes							
Aetna Whole Health-Out-Network	40%/40%	40%	40%	40%/40%	No							
Dean Health Plan-High	$10/$10	None	$10	50%/$75max/50%	Yes	71.2	87.8	87.4	94	85.8	85.8	66
Group Health Cooperative-High	$10/$10	None	$5	$20/$20	Yes	81.1	83.6	87.2	95.1	93.1	94.4	74.6
HealthPartners-High-Option	$25/$45	Nothing	$12	$45/$90	Yes	60.3	85.7	88.2	97.8	90	89.2	68.9
HealthPartners-Std-Option	$0 for 3, then 20%	20% In/40% out	$9	$40/$70	Yes	60.3	85.7	88.2	97.8	90	89.2	68.9
MercyCare HMO-High	$10/$10	Nothing	$10	$20/$50	Yes	76.7	89.6	85.1	94.5	89.9	86.6	70
Physicians Plus-High	$10/$10	Nothing	$10	30%/50%	No	75.9	77.9	86.3	94.6	89.2	91.1	71.4
Wyoming												
Aetna Value Plan	$25/$40	20%	$10	30%/50%	Yes							
Altius Health Plans-High	$20/$30	$200	$7	$25/$50	Yes	60.8	86.5	89.6	94.7	82.1	88.3	60.7
Altius Health Plans-Std	$20/$35	None	$7	$35/$60	Yes	60.8	86.5	89.6	94.7	82.1	88.3	60.7

Appendix E
FEHB Plan Comparison Charts

High Deductible and Consumer-Driven Health Plans
With a Health Savings Account or Health Reimbursement Arrangement
(Pages 74 through 93)

A High Deductible Health Plan (HDHP) provides comprehensive coverage for high-cost medical events and a tax-advantaged way to help you build savings for future medical expenses. The HDHP gives you greater flexibility and discretion over how you use your health care benefits.

When you enroll, your health plan establishes for you either a Health Savings Account (HSA) or a Health Reimbursement Arrangement (HRA). The plan automatically deposits the monthly "premium pass through" into your HSA. The plan credits an amount into the HRA. (This is the "Premium Contribution to HSA/HRA" column in the following charts.)

Preventive care is covered in full. As you receive other non-preventive medical care, you must meet the plan deductible before the health plan pays benefits. You can choose to pay your deductible with funds from your HSA or you can choose instead to pay for your deductible out-of-pocket, allowing your savings to continue to grow.

The HDHP features higher annual deductibles (a minimum of $1,250 for Self Only and $2,500 for Self and Family coverage) and annual out-of-pocket limits (not to exceed $6,250 for Self Only and $12,500 for Self and Family coverage) than other insurance plans. Depending on the HDHP you choose, you may have the choice of using In-Network and Out-of-Network providers. There may be higher deductibles and out-of-pocket limits when you use Out-of-Network providers. Using In-Network providers will save you money.

Health Savings Account (HSA)

A Health Savings Account allows individuals to pay for current health expenses and save for future qualified medical expenses on a pre-tax basis. Funds deposited into an HSA are not taxed, the balance in the HSA grows tax free, and that amount is available on a tax free basis to pay medical costs. You are eligible for an HSA if you are enrolled in an HDHP, not covered by any other health plan that is not an HDHP (including a spouse's health plan, but does not include specific injury insurance and accident, disability, dental care, vision care, or long-term coverage), not enrolled in Medicare, not received VA benefits or IHS benefits within the last three months, not covered by your own or your spouse's flexible spending account (FSA), and are not claimed as a dependent on someone else's tax return. If you are enrolled in a High Deductible Health Plan with an HSA you may not participate in a Health Care Flexible Spending Account (HCFSA), but you are permitted to participate in a Limited Expense (LEX) HCFSA. HSAs are subject to a number of rules and limitations established by the Department of the Treasury.

Visit www.ustreas.gov/offices/public-affairs/hsa for more information. The 2013 maximum contribution limits are $3,250 for Self Only coverage and $6,450 for Self and Family coverage. If you are over 55, you can make an additional "catch up" contribution. You can use funds in your account to help pay your health plan deductible.

Appendix E
FEHB Plan Comparison Charts

High Deductible and Consumer-Driven Health Plans
With a Health Savings Account or Health Reimbursement Arrangement

Features of an HSA include:

- Tax-deductible deposits you make to the HSA. Your own HSA contributions are either tax-deductible or pre-tax (if made by payroll deduction). See IRS Publication 969.
- Tax-deferred interest earned on the account.
- Tax-free withdrawals for qualified medical expenses.
- Carryover of unused funds and interest from year to year.
- Portability; the account is owned by you and is yours to keep – even when you retire, leave government service, or change plans.

Health Reimbursement Arrangement (HRA)

Health Reimbursement Arrangements are a common feature of Consumer-Driven Health Plans. They may be referred to by the health plan under a different name, such as personal care account. They are also available to enrollees in High Deductible Health Plans who are not eligible for an HSA. HRAs are similar to HSAs except:

- An enrollee cannot make deposits into an HRA;
- A health plan may impose a ceiling on the value of an HRA;
- Interest is not earned on an HRA; and
- The amount in an HRA is not transferable if the enrollee leaves the health plan.

If you are enrolled in a High Deductible Health Plan with an HRA you may participate in a Health Care Flexible Spending Account (HCFSA).

The plan will credit the HRA different amounts depending on whether you have a Self Only or a Self and Family enrollment. You can use funds in your account to help pay your health plan deductible.

Features of an HRA include:

- Tax-free withdrawals for qualified medical expenses.
- Carryover of unused credits from year to year.
- Credits in an HRA do not earn interest.
- Credits in the HRA are forfeited if you leave federal employment or switch health insurance plans

Appendix E
FEHB Plan Comparison Charts

High Deductible and Consumer-Driven Health Plans
With a Health Savings Account or Health Reimbursement Arrangement

	Health Savings Account (HSA)	Health Reimbursement Arrangement (HRA)
ELIGIBILITY	You must enroll in a High Deductible Health Plan (HDHP). No other general medical insurance coverage is permitted. You cannot be enrolled in Medicare Part A or Part B. You cannot be claimed as a dependent on someone else's tax returns.	You must enroll in a High Deductible Health Plan (HDHP).
FUNDING	The plan deposits a monthly "premium pass through" into your account.	The plan deposits the credit amount directly into your account.
CONTRIBUTIONS	The maximum allowed is a combination of the health plan "premium pass through" and the member contribution up to the maximum contribution amount set by the IRS each year.	Only that portion of the premium specified by the health plan will be contributed. You cannot add your own money to an HRA.
DISTRIBUTIONS	May be used to pay the out-of-pocket medical expenses for yourself, your spouse, or your dependents (even if they are not covered by the HDHP), or to pay the plan's deductible. See IRS Publication 502 for a complete list of eligible expenses.	May be used to pay the out-of-pocket expenses for qualified medical expenses for individuals covered under the HDHP, or to pay the plan's deductible. See IRS Publication 502 for a complete list of eligible expenses.
PORTABLE	Yes, you can take this account with you when you change plans, separate from service, or retire.	If you retire and remain in your HDHP you may continue to use and accumulate credits in your HRA. If you terminate employment or change health plans, only eligible expenses incurred while covered under that HDHP will be eligible for reimbursement, subject to timely filing requirements. Unused credits are forfeited.
ANNUAL ROLLOVER	Yes, funds accumulate without a maximum cap.	Yes, credits accumulate without a maximum cap.

IMPORTANT REMINDER: This is only a summary of the features of the HDHP/HSA or HRA. Refer to the specific Plan brochure for the complete details covering Plan design, operation, and administration as each Plan will have differences.

Appendix E
FEHB Plan Comparison Charts

High Deductible and Consumer-Driven Health Plans
With a Health Savings Account or Health Reimbursement Arrangement

The tables on the following pages highlight selected features that may help you narrow your choice of health plans. The tables do not show all of your possible out-of-pocket costs. All benefits are subject to the definitions, limitations, and exclusions set forth in each plan's Federal brochure which is the official statement of benefits available under the plan's contract with the Office of Personnel Management. Always consult plan brochures before making your final decision.

A Consumer-Driven plan provides you with freedom in spending health care dollars the way you want. The typical plan has features such as: member responsibility for certain up-front medical costs, an employer-funded account that you may use to pay these up-front costs, and catastrophic coverage with a high deductible. You and your family receive full coverage for In-Network preventive care.

Appendix E
FEHB Plan Comparison Charts

High Deductible and Consumer-Driven Health Plans
With a Health Savings Account or Health Reimbursement Arrangement

The tables on the following pages highlight what you are expected to pay for selected features under each plan. The charts are not a complete statement of your out-of-pocket obligations in every individual circumstance. Unlike many regular medical plans, the covered out-of-pocket expenses under a High Deductible Health Plan, including office visit copayments and prescription drug copayments, count toward the calendar year deductible and the catastrophic limit. *You must read the plan's brochure for details.*

Premium Contribution (pass through) to HSA/HRA (or personal care account) shows the amount your health plan automatically deposits or credits into your account on a monthly basis for Self Only/Self and Family enrollments. (Consumer-Driven Health Plans credit accounts annually.) The amount credited under "Premium Contribution" is shown as a monthly amount for comparison purposes only.

Calendar Year (CY) Deductible Self/Family is the maximum amount of covered expenses an individual or family must pay out-of-pocket, including deductibles, coinsurance and copayments, before the plan pays catastrophic benefits.

Catastrophic (Cat.) Limit Self/Family is the maximum amount of covered expenses an individual or family must pay out-of-pocket, including deductibles and coinsurance and copays, before the Plan pays catastrophic benefits.

Office Visit shows what you pay for a visit to a primary care physician after the deductible is met for other than preventive care.

Inpatient Hospital shows what you pay after the deductible is met for hospital services when an inpatient. The amount could be a daily copayment up to a specified amount (e.g., $50 a day up to three days), a coinsurance amount such as

Plan Name	Telephone Number	Enrollment Code		Your Share of Premium		Your Share of Premium	
		Self only	Self & family	Self only	Self & family	Self only	Self & family
APWU Health Plan -CDHP - Nationwide	800-718-1299	474	475	94.58	212.77	43.65	98.20
GEHA High Deductible Health Plan -HDHP - Nationwide	800-821-6136	341	342	104.96	239.74	48.44	110.65
MHBP Consumer Option -HDHP- Nationwide	800-694-9901	481	482	134.40	304.55	62.03	140.56

The information contained in this Guide is not the official statement of benefits. Each plan's Federal brochure is the official statement of benefits.

Appendix E
FEHB Plan Comparison Charts

High Deductible and Consumer-Driven Health Plans
With a Health Savings Account or Health Reimbursement Arrangement

20%, or a flat deductible amount (e.g., $200 per admission). This amount does not include charges from physicians or for services that may not be charged by the hospital such as laboratory or radiology.

Outpatient Surgery shows what you pay the doctor for surgery performed on an outpatient basis.

Preventive Services are often covered in full, usually with no or only a small deductible or copayment. Preventive services may also be payable up to an annual maximum dollar amount (e.g., up to $300 per person per year).

Prescription Drugs are categorized using a variety of terms to define what you pay such as generic, brand, Level I, Level II, Tier I, Tier II, etc. In capturing these differences we use the following: **Level I** includes most generic drugs, but may include some preferred brands. **Level II** may include generics and preferred brands not included in Level I. **Level III** includes all other covered drugs with some exceptions for specialty drugs. The level in which a medication is placed and what you pay for prescription drugs is often based on what the plan is charged.

High Deductible Health Plans and Consumer Driven Health Plans are much different from the other types of plans shown in this Guide. You can use in-network providers to save money. If you use out-of-network providers, however, you not only pay more of the costs but you are also usually responsible for any difference between the amount billed for a service and what the plan actually allows. (For example, you receive a bill from an out-of-network provider for $100 but the plan allows $85 for the service. You pay the higher copayment for out-of-network care plus the $15 difference between $100 – the billed amount – and the plan's allowance of $85.) In addition, the difference you pay between the billed amount and the plan's allowance does not count toward satisfying the catastrophic limit.

Plan Name	Benefit Type	Premium Contribution Self/Family	CY Ded. Self/Family	Cat. Limit Self/Family	Office Visit	Inpatient Hospital	Outpatient Surgery	Preventive Services	Prescription Drugs Levels I, II, III
APWU Health Plan-	In-Network	$1200/$2400	$600/$1,200	$3,000/$4,500	15%	None	15%	Nothing	25%/25%/25%
APWU Health Plan-	Out-Network	$1200/$2400	$600/$1,200	$9,000/$9,000	40%+diff.	None	40%+diff.	Nothing up to $1200	Not Covered/N/A/N/A
GEHA HDHP-	In-Network	$62.50/$125	$1,500/$3,000	$5,000/$10,000	5%	5%	5%	Nothing	25%/25%/25%
GEHA HDHP-	Out-Network	$62.50/$125	$1,500/$3,000	$5,000/$10,000	25%	25%	25%	Ded/25%	25%+/25%+/25%+
MHBP Consumer Option-	In-Network	$70/$141	$2,000/$4,000	$5,000/$10,000	$15	$75 day-$750	Nothing	Nothing	$10/$25/$40
MHBP Consumer Option-	Out-Network	$70/$141	$2,000/$4,000	$7,500/$15,000	40%	40%	40%	Not Covered	Not Covered

High Deductible Health Plans and Consumer-Driven Health Plan Member Survey Results

Member Survey results are collected, scored, and reported by an independent organization – not by the health plans. See Appendix D for a fuller explanation of each survey category.

Overall Plan Satisfaction	• How would you rate your overall experience with your health plan?
Getting Needed Care	• How often was it easy to get an appointment, the care, tests, or treatment you thought you needed through your health plan?
Getting Care Quickly	• When you needed care right away, how often did you get care as soon as you thought you needed? • Not counting the times you needed care right away, how often did you get an appointment at a doctor's office or clinic as soon as you thought you needed?
How Well Doctors Communicate	• How often did your personal doctor explain things in a way that was easy to understand? • How often did your personal doctor listen carefully to you, show respect for what you had to say, and spend enough time with you?
Customer Service	• How often did written materials or the Internet provide the information you needed about how your health plan works? • How often did your health plan's customer service give you the information or help you needed? • How often were the forms from your health plan easy to fill out?
Claims Processing	• How often did your health plan handle your claims quickly and correctly?
Plan Information on Costs	• How often were you able to find out from your health plan how much you would have to pay for a health care service or equipment, or for specific prescription drug medicines?

Member Survey Results

High Deductible Health Plans

Plan Name	Plan Code	Overall plan satisfaction	Getting needed care	Getting care quickly	How well doctors communicate	Customer service	Claims processing	Plan Information on Costs
HDHP National Average		**63.3**	**86**	**88.8**	**94.1**	**83.1**	**88**	**60.4**
Aetna Health Fund - Nationwide	22	68.1	88.2	86.9	93.9	82.7	85.7	60
GEHA High Deductible Health Plan - Nationwide	34	64.7	84.2	88.8	93.6	82.9	90.2	59.4
MHBP Consumer Option - Nationwide	48	57.1	85.5	90.7	94.8	83.6	88.2	61.8

Consumer-Driven Health Plans

Plan Name	Plan Code	Overall plan satisfaction	Getting needed care	Getting care quickly	How well doctors communicate	Customer service	Claims processing	Plan Information on Costs
CDHP National Average		**56.4**	**85.1**	**86**	**93.5**	**82.7**	**85.7**	**60.6**
Aetna Health Fund - Nationwide	22	68.1	88.2	86.9	93.9	82.7	85.7	60
APWU Health Plan - Nationwide	47	64.6	88.5	89.3	91.3	77.7	82.9	66.9
Humana Coverage First -TX	TP,TU,TV	64.5	83.7	84.3	93.5	81.8	84	55.7
Humana Coverage First - KS, MO	PH	44.1	81.6	88.8	95.9	88.4	90.6	63.6

The tables on the following pages highlight selected features that may help you narrow your choice of health plans. The tables do not show all of your possible out-of-pocket costs. All benefits are subject to the definitions, limitations, and exclusions set forth in each plan's Federal brochure which is the official statement of benefits available under the plan's contract with the Office of Personnel Management. Always consult plan brochures before making your final decision.

High Deductible and Consumer-Driven Health Plans

See pages 74-75 for an explanation of the columns on these pages.

Plan Name	Telephone Number	Enrollment Code		Your Share of Premium			
				Monthly		Biweekly	
		Self only	Self & family	Self only	Self & family	Self only	Self & family
Aetna HealthFund -CDHP-AK, CA,HI,IN, OH, OK, SC, TX, & WI	877-459-6604	221	222	185.23	438.90	85.49	202.57
Aetna HealthFund -HDHP- All 50 States and DC	877-459-6604	224	225	103.76	227.22	47.89	104.87

Plan Name	Telephone Number	Enrollment Code		Your Share of Premium			
				Monthly		Biweekly	
		Self only	Self & family	Self only	Self & family	Self only	Self & family
Alabama							
Aetna Healthfund CDHP-Most of Alabama	877-459-6604	F51	F52	158.71	378.69	73.25	174.78
Arizona							
Aetna Healthfund CDHP-All of Arizona	877-459-6604	G51	G52	167.35	398.34	77.24	183.85
Arkansas							
Aetna Healthfund CDHP-Most of Arkansas	877-459-6604	F51	F52	158.71	378.69	73.25	174.78
Colorado							
Aetna Healthfund CDHP-All of Colorado	877-459-6604	G51	G52	167.35	398.34	77.24	183.85
Connecticut							
Aetna Healthfund CDHP-All of Connecticut	877-459-6604	EP1	EP2	184.12	436.38	84.98	201.41

The information contained in this Guide is not the official statement of benefits. Each plan's Federal brochure is the official statement of benefits.

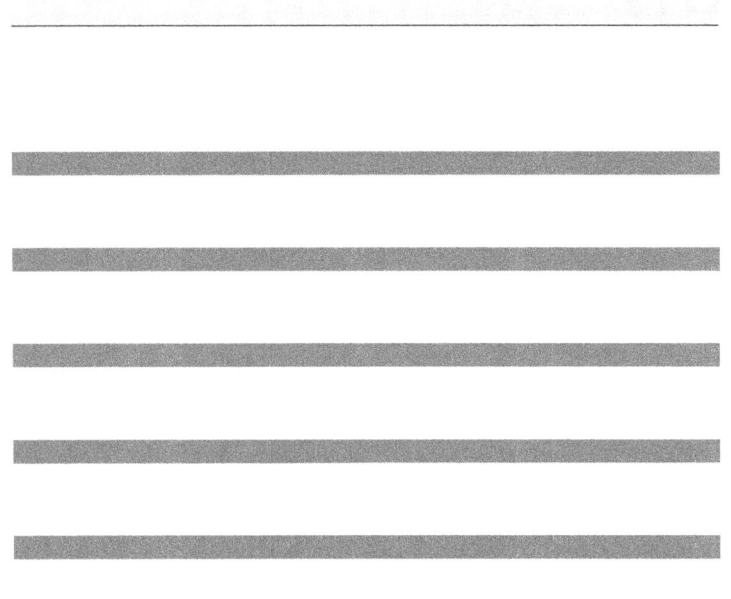

Plan Name	Benefit Type	Premium Contribution to HSA/HRA	CY Ded. Self/Family	Cat. Limit Self/Family	Office Visit	Inpatient Hospital	Outpatient Surgery	Preventive Services	Prescription Drugs Levels I, II, III
Aetna HealthFund-In-Network		$83.33/166.66	$1,000/$2,000	$5,000/$10,000	20%	20%	20%	Nothing	$10/30%/50%
Aetna HealthFund-Out-Network		$83.33/166.66	$1,000/$2,000	$6,000/$12,000	40%	40%	40%	Fund/Ded/40%	40%+/30%+/50%+
Aetna HealthFund-In-Network		$62.50/$125	$1,500/$3,000	$4,000/$8,000	10%	10%	10%	Nothing	$10/$35/$60
Aetna HealthFund-Out-Network		$62.50/$125	$2,500/$5,000	$5,000/$10,000	30%	30%	30%	Ded/30%	30%+/30%+/30%+

Plan Name	Benefit Type	Premium Contribution to HSA/HRA	CY Ded. Self/Family	Cat. Limit Self/Family	Office Visit	Inpatient Hospital	Outpatient Surgery	Preventive Services	Prescription Drugs Levels I, II, III
Alabama									
Aetna Healthfund CDHP-In-Network		$83.33/$166.66	$1,000/$2,000	$4,000/$8,000	15%	15%	15%	Nothing	$10/$35/$60
Aetna Healthfund CDHP-Out-Network		$83.33/$166.66	$1,000/$2,000	$5,000/$10,000	40%	40%	40%	Fund/Ded/40%	40%/40%+/40%+
Arizona									
Aetna Healthfund CDHP-In-Network		$83.33/$166.66	$1,000/$2,000	$4,000/$8,000	15%	15%	15%	Nothing	$10/$35/$60
Aetna Healthfund CDHP-Out-Network		$83.33/$166.66	$1,000/$2,000	$5,000/$10,000	40%	40%	40%	Fund/Ded/40%	40%/40%+/40%+
Arkansas									
Aetna Healthfund CDHP-In-Network		$83.33/$166.66	$1,000/$2,000	$4,000/$8,000	15%	15%	15%	Nothing	$10/$35/$60
Aetna Healthfund CDHP-Out-Network		$83.33/$166.66	$1,000/$2,000	$5,000/$10,000	40%	40%	40%	Fund/Ded/40%	40%/40%+/40%+
Colorado									
Aetna Healthfund CDHP-In-Network		$83.33/$166.66	$1,000/$2,000	$4,000/$8,000	15%	15%	15%	Nothing	$10/$35/$60
Aetna Healthfund CDHP-Out-Network		$83.33/$166.66	$1,000/$2,000	$5,000/$10,000	40%	40%	40%	Fund/Ded/40%	40%/40%+/40%+
Connecticut									
Aetna Healthfund CDHP-In-Network		$83.33/$166.66	$1,000/$2,000	$4,000/$8,000	15%	15%	15%	Nothing	$10/$35/$60
Aetna Healthfund CDHP-Out-Network		$83.33/$166.66	$1,000/$2,000	$5,000/$10,000	40%	40%	40%	Fund/Ded/40%	40%/40%+/40%+

High Deductible and Consumer-Driven Health Plans

See pages 74-75 for an explanation of the columns on these pages.

| Plan Name | Telephone Number | Enrollment Code | | Your Share of Premium | | | |
| | | | | Monthly | | Biweekly | |
		Self only	Self & family	Self only	Self & family	Self only	Self & family
Delaware							
Aetna Healthfund CDHP-All of Delaware	877-459-6604	EP1	EP2	184.12	436.38	84.98	201.41
District of Columbia							
Aetna Healthfund CDHP-All of Washington D.C.	877-459-6604	F51	F52	158.71	378.69	73.25	174.78
CareFirst BlueChoice-HDHP-Washington D.C. Metro Area	888-789-9065	B61	B62	127.44	284.25	58.82	131.19
Florida							
Aetna Healthfund CDHP-Most of Florida	877-459-6604	F51	F52	158.71	378.69	73.25	174.78
Coventry Health Care of Florida -HDHP-Southern Florida	800-441-5501	J41	J42	129.79	367.55	59.90	169.64
Humana CoverageFirst -CDHP- Tampa Area	888-393-6765	MJ1	MJ2	129.31	287.72	59.68	132.79
Humana CoverageFirst -CDHP- South Florida Area	888-393-6765	QP1	QP2	110.84	246.62	51.16	113.82
Georgia							
Aetna Healthfund CDHP-All of Georgia	877-459-6604	F51	F52	158.71	378.69	73.25	174.78
Humana CoverageFirst -CDHP- Atlanta Area	888-393-6765	AD1	AD2	117.00	260.31	54.00	120.14
Humana CoverageFirst -CDHP- Macon Area	888-393-6765	LM1	LM2	123.15	274.02	56.84	126.47
Guam							
TakeCare -HDHP- Guam/N. Mariana Islands/Belau (Palau)	671-647-3526	KX1	KX2	74.90	196.74	34.57	90.80
Idaho							
Aetna Healthfund CDHP-Most of Idaho	877-459-6604	H41	H42	157.86	376.78	72.86	173.90
Altius Health Plans -HDHP- Southern Region	800-377-4161	9K4	9K5	87.04	180.33	40.17	83.23

The information contained in this Guide is not the official statement of benefits. Each plan's Federal brochure is the official statement of benefits.

Plan Name	Benefit Type	Premium Contribution to HSA/HRA	CY Ded. Self/Family	Cat. Limit Self/Family	Office Visit	Inpatient Hospital	Outpatient Surgery	Preventive Services	Prescription Drugs Levels I, II, III
Delaware									
Aetna Healthfund CDHP-In-Network		$83.33/$166.66	$1,000/$2,000	$4,000/$8,000	15%	15%	15%	Nothing	$10/$35/$60
Aetna Healthfund CDHP-Out-Network		$83.33/$166.66	$1,000/$2,000	$5,000/$10,000	40%	40%	40%	Fund/Ded/40%	40%/40%+/40%+
District of Columbia									
Aetna Healthfund CDHP-In-Network		$83.33/$166.66	$1,000/$2,000	$4,000/$8,000	15%	15%	15%	Nothing	$10/$35/$60
Aetna Healthfund CDHP-Out-Network		$83.33/$166.66	$1,000/$2,000	$5,000/$10,000	40%	40%	40%	Fund/Ded/40%	40%/40%+/40%+
CareFirst BlueChoice		$37.50/$75.00	$1500/$3000	$4000/$8000	Nothing	$300	Nothing	Nothing	0/$25/$45
CareFirst BlueChoice-Out of Network		$37.50/$75.00	$3000/$6000	$6000/$12000	$70	$500	$70	Ded, then Nothing	0/$25/$45
Florida									
Aetna Healthfund CDHP-In-Network		$83.33/$166.66	$1,000/$2,000	$4,000/$8,000	15%	15%	15%	Nothing	$10/$35/$60
Aetna Healthfund CDHP-Out-Network		$83.33/$166.66	$1,000/$2,000	$5,000/$10,000	40%	40%	40%	Fund/Ded/40%	40%/40%+/40%+
Coventry Health Care of Florida		$83.34/$166.67	$2,500/$5,000	$5,000/$10,000	$10	Ded+20%	Ded+20%	Nothing	$5/$35/$50/20%
Humana CoverageFirst-In-Network		$83.33	$1,000/$2,000	$3,000/$6,000	$25	$300/day x 5	$150	Nothing	$10/$40/$60
Humana CoverageFirst-Out-Network		N/A	$3,000/$6,000	$4,000/$8,000	30%	30%	30%	30%	$10+/$40+/$60+
Humana CoverageFirst-In-Network		$83.33	$1,000/$2,000	$3,000/$6,000	$25	$300/day x 5	$150	Nothing	$10/$40/$60
Humana CoverageFirst-Out-Network		N/A	$3,000/$6,000	$4,000/$8,000	30%	30%	30%	30%	$10+/$40+/$60+
Georgia									
Aetna Healthfund CDHP-In-Network		$83.33/$166.66	$1,000/$2,000	$4,000/$8,000	15%	15%	15%	Nothing	$10/$35/$60
Aetna Healthfund CDHP-Out-Network		$83.33/$166.66	$1,000/$2,000	$5,000/$10,000	40%	40%	40%	Fund/Ded/40%	40%/40%+/40%+
Humana CoverageFirst-In-Network		$83.33	$1,000/$2,000	$3,000/$6,000	$25	$300/day x 5	$150	Nothing	$10/$40/$60
Humana CoverageFirst-Out-Network		N/A	$3,000/$6,000	$4,000/$8,000	30%	30%	30%	30%	$10+/$40+/$60+
Humana CoverageFirst-In-Network		$83.33	$1,000/$2,000	$3,000/$6,000	$25	$300/day x 5	$150	Nothing	$10/$40/$60
Humana CoverageFirst-Out-Network		N/A	$3,000/$6,000	$4,000/$8,000	30%	30%	30%	30%	$10+/$40+/$60+
Guam									
TakeCare- In-Network		$71.50/$186.33	$3,000/$6,000	$5,000/$10,000	20% after Ded	20% after Ded	20% after Ded	Nothing	$20/$40/$80
TakeCare- Out-Network		$71.50/$186.33	$3,000/$6,000	$10,000/$20,000	30% after Ded	30% after Ded	30% after Ded	1st $300/ded	30% after Ded
Idaho									
Aetna Healthfund CDHP-In-Network		$83.33/$166.66	$1,000/$2,000	$4,000/$8,000	15%	15%	15%	Nothing	$10/$35/$60
Aetna Healthfund CDHP-Out-Network		$83.33/$166.66	$1,000/$2,000	$5,000/$10,000	40%	40%	40%	Fund/Ded/40%	40%/40%+/40%+
Altius Health Plans		$45.83/$91.66	$1,250/$2,500	$5,000/$10,000	$20	10%	10%	Nothing	$7/$25/$50

High Deductible and Consumer-Driven Health Plans

See pages 74-75 for an explanation of the columns on these pages.

| Plan Name | Telephone Number | Enrollment Code | | Your Share of Premium | | | |
| | | | | Monthly | | Biweekly | |
		Self only	Self & family	Self only	Self & family	Self only	Self & family
Illinois							
Aetna Healthfund CDHP-Most of Illinois	877-459-6604	H41	H42	157.86	376.78	72.86	173.90
Humana CoverageFirst -CDHP- Central Illinois	888-393-6765	GB1	GB2	129.31	287.72	59.68	132.79
Humana CoverageFirst -CDHP- Chicago Area	888-393-6765	MW1	MW2	123.15	274.02	56.84	126.47
Indiana							
Humana CoverageFirst -CDHP- Lake/Porter/LaPorte Counties	888-393-6765	MW1	MW2	123.15	274.02	56.84	126.47
Iowa							
Aetna Healthfund CDHP-All of Iowa	877-459-6604	H41	H42	157.86	376.78	72.86	173.90
Coventry Health Care of Iowa -HDHP- Central/Eastern/Western Iowa	800-257-4692	SV4	SV5	89.68	214.02	41.39	98.78
Kansas							
Aetna Healthfund CDHP-Most of Kansas	877-459-6604	G51	G52	167.35	398.34	77.24	183.85
Coventry Health Care of Kansas (Kansas City)-HDHP- Kansas City Metro Area (KS and MO)	800-969-3343	9H1	9H2	106.04	249.19	48.94	115.01
Humana CoverageFirst -CDHP- Kansas City Area	888-393-6765	PH1	PH2	110.84	246.62	51.16	113.82
Kentucky							
Aetna Healthfund CDHP-Most of Kentucky	877-459-6604	H41	H42	157.86	376.78	72.86	173.90
Humana CoverageFirst -CDHP- Lexington Area	888-393-6765	6N1	6N2	111.02	247.03	51.24	114.01
Louisiana							
Aetna Healthfund CDHP-Most of Louisiana	877-459-6604	F51	F52	158.71	378.69	73.25	174.78

The information contained in this Guide is not the official statement of benefits. Each plan's Federal brochure is the official statement of benefits.

Plan Name	Benefit Type	Premium Contribution to HSA/HRA	CY Ded. Self/Family	Cat. Limit Self/Family	Office Visit	Inpatient Hospital	Outpatient Surgery	Preventive Services	Prescription Drugs Levels I, II, III
Illinois									
Aetna Healthfund CDHP-In-Network		$83.33/$166.66	$1,000/$2,000	$4,000/$8,000	15%	15%	15%	Nothing	$10/$35/$60
Aetna Healthfund CDHP-Out-Network		$83.33/$166.66	$1,000/$2,000	$5,000/$10,000	40%	40%	40%	Fund/Ded/40%	40%/40%+/40%+
Humana CoverageFirst-In-Network		$83.33	$1,000/$2,000	$3,000/$6,000	$25	$300/day x 5	$150	Nothing	$10/$40/$60
Humana CoverageFirst-Out-Network		N/A	$3,000/$6,000	$4,000/$8,000	30%	30%	30%	30%	$10+/$40+/$60+
Humana CoverageFirst-In-Network		$83.33	$1,000/$2,000	$3,000/$6,000	$25	$300/day x 5	$150	Nothing	$10/$40/$60
Humana CoverageFirst-Out-Network		N/A	$3,000/$6,000	$4,000/$8,000	30%	30%	30%	30%	$10+/$40+/$60+
Indiana									
Humana CoverageFirst-In-Network		$83.33	$1,000/$2,000	$3,000/$6,000	$25	$300/day x 5	$150	Nothing	$10/$40/$60
Humana CoverageFirst-Out-Network		N/A	$3,000/$6,000	$4,000/$8,000	30%	30%	30%	30%	$10+/$40+/$60+
Iowa									
Aetna Healthfund CDHP-In-Network		$83.33/$166.66	$1,000/$2,000	$4,000/$8,000	15%	15%	15%	Nothing	$10/$35/$60
Aetna Healthfund CDHP-Out-Network		$83.33/$166.66	$1,000/$2,000	$5,000/$10,000	40%	40%	40%	Fund/Ded/40%	40%/40%/40%+
Coventry Health Care of Iowa		$66.67/$133.34	$2,100/$4,200	$5,000/$10,000	$20	15%	15%	Nothing	$3/$10/$40/$65
Kansas									
Aetna Healthfund CDHP-In-Network		$83.33/$166.66	$1,000/$2,000	$4,000/$8,000	15%	15%	15%	Nothing	$10/$35/$60
Aetna Healthfund CDHP-Out-Network		$83.33/$166.66	$1,000/$2,000	$5,000/$10,000	40%	40%	40%	Fund/Ded/40%	40%/40%+/40%+
Coventry Health Care of Kansas (Kansas City)-HDHP		$83.33/$166.66	$2,500/$5,000	$3,500/$7,000	20%	20%	20%	Nothing	20%/20%/20%
Humana CoverageFirst-In-Network		$83.33	$1,000/$2,000	$3,000/$6,000	$25	$300/day x 5	$150	Nothing	$10/$40/$60
Humana CoverageFirst-Out-Network		N/A	$3,000/$6,000	$4,000/$8,000	30%	30%	30%	30%	$10+/$40+/$60+
Kentucky									
Aetna Healthfund CDHP-In-Network		$83.33/$166.66	$1,000/$2,000	$4,000/$8,000	15%	15%	15%	Nothing	$10/$35/$60
Aetna Healthfund CDHP-Out-Network		$83.33/$166.66	$1,000/$2,000	$5,000/$10,000	40%	40%	40%	Fund/Ded/40%	40%/40%+/40%+
Humana CoverageFirst-In-Network		$83.33	$1,000/$2,000	$3,000/$6,000	$25	$300/day x 5	$150	Nothing	$10/$40/$60
Humana CoverageFirst-Out-Network		N/A	$3,000/$6,000	$4,000/$8,000	30%	30%	30%	30%	$10+/$40+/$60+
Louisiana									
Aetna Healthfund CDHP-In-Network		$83.33/$166.66	$1,000/$2,000	$4,000/$8,000	15%	15%	15%	Nothing	$10/$35/$60
Aetna Healthfund CDHP-Out-Network		$83.33/$166.66	$1,000/$2,000	$5,000/$10,000	40%	40%	40%	Fund/Ded/40%	40%/40%+/40%+

High Deductible and Consumer-Driven Health Plans

See pages 74-75 for an explanation of the columns on these pages.

| Plan Name | Telephone Number | Enrollment Code | | Your Share of Premium | | | |
| | | | | Monthly | | Biweekly | |
		Self only	Self & family	Self only	Self & family	Self only	Self & family
Maine							
Aetna Healthfund CDHP-All of Maine	877-459-6604	EP1	EP2	184.12	436.38	84.98	201.41
Maryland							
Aetna Healthfund CDHP-All of Maryland	877-459-6604	F51	F52	158.71	378.69	73.25	174.78
CareFirst BlueChoice-HDHP-All of Maryland	888-789-9065	B61	B62	127.44	284.25	58.82	131.19
Coventry Health Care -HDHP- All of Maryland	800-833-7423	GZ1	GZ2	118.94	269.20	54.90	124.24
Massachusetts							
Aetna Healthfund CDHP-Most of Massachusetts	877-459-6604	EP1	EP2	184.12	436.38	84.98	201.41
Michigan							
Aetna Healthfund CDHP-All of Michigan	877-459-6604	G51	G52	167.35	398.34	77.24	183.85
Minnesota							
Aetna Healthfund CDHP-Most of Minnesota	877-459-6604	H41	H42	157.86	376.78	72.86	173.90
Mississippi							
Aetna Healthfund CDHP-Most of Mississippi	877-459-6604	H41	H42	157.86	376.78	72.86	173.90
Missouri							
Aetna Healthfund CDHP-Most of Missouri	877-459-6604	G51	G52	167.35	398.34	77.24	183.85
Coventry Health Care of Kansas (Kansas City)-HDHP- Kansas City Metro Area (KS and MO)	800-969-3343	9H1	9H2	106.04	249.19	48.94	115.01
Humana CoverageFirst -CDHP- Kansas City Area	888-393-6765	PH1	PH2	110.84	246.62	51.16	113.82

The information contained in this Guide is not the official statement of benefits. Each plan's Federal brochure is the official statement of benefits.

Plan Name	Benefit Type	Premium Contribution to HSA/HRA	CY Ded. Self/Family	Cat. Limit Self/Family	Office Visit	Inpatient Hospital	Outpatient Surgery	Preventive Services	Prescription Drugs Levels I, II, III
Maine									
Aetna Healthfund CDHP-In-Network		$83.33/$166.66	$1,000/$2,000	$4,000/$8,000	15%	15%	15%	Nothing	$10/$35/$60
Aetna Healthfund CDHP-Out-Network		$83.33/$166.66	$1,000/$2,000	$5,000/$10,000	40%	40%	40%	Fund/Ded/40%	40%/40%+/40%+
Maryland									
Aetna Healthfund CDHP-In-Network		$83.33/$166.66	$1,000/$2,000	$4,000/$8,000	15%	15%	15%	Nothing	$10/$35/$60
Aetna Healthfund CDHP-Out-Network		$83.33/$166.66	$1,000/$2,000	$5,000/$10,000	40%	40%	40%	Fund/Ded/40%	40%/40%+/40%+
CareFirst BlueChoice-In-Network		$37.50/$75.00	$1500/$3000	$4000/$8000	Nothing	$300	Nothing	Nothing	0/$25/$45
CareFirst BlueChoice-Out-Network		$37.50/$75.00	$3000/$6000	$6000/$12000	$70	$500	$70	Ded, then Nothing	0/$25/$45
Coventry Health Care HDHP -In-Network		$41.67/$83.34	$2,000/$4,000	$4,000/$8,000	$15	Nothing	Nothing	Nothing	#3/$15/$30/$60
Coventry Health Care HDHP -Out-Network		$41.67/$83.34	$2,000/$4,000	$4,000/$8,000	30%	30%	30%	30%	N/A
Massachusetts									
Aetna Healthfund CDHP-In-Network		$83.33/$166.66	$1,000/$2,000	$4,000/$8,000	15%	15%	15%	Nothing	$10/$35/$60
Aetna Healthfund CDHP-Out-Network		$83.33/$166.66	$1,000/$2,000	$5,000/$10,000	40%	40%	40%	Fund/Ded/40%	40%/40%+/40%+
Michigan									
Aetna Healthfund CDHP-In-Network		$83.33/$166.66	$1,000/$2,000	$4,000/$8,000	15%	15%	15%	Nothing	$10/$35/$60
Aetna Healthfund CDHP-Out-Network		$83.33/$166.66	$1,000/$2,000	$5,000/$10,000	40%	40%	40%	Fund/Ded/40%	40%/40%+/40%+
Minnesota									
Aetna Healthfund CDHP-In-Network		$83.33/$166.66	$1,000/$2,000	$4,000/$8,000	15%	15%	15%	Nothing	$10/$35/$60
Aetna Healthfund CDHP-Out-Network		$83.33/$166.66	$1,000/$2,000	$5,000/$10,000	40%	40%	40%	Fund/Ded/40%	40%/40%+/40%+
Mississippi									
Aetna Healthfund CDHP-In-Network		$83.33/$166.66	$1,000/$2,000	$4,000/$8,000	15%	15%	15%	Nothing	$10/$35/$60
Aetna Healthfund CDHP-Out-Network		$83.33/$166.66	$1,000/$2,000	$5,000/$10,000	40%	40%	40%	Fund/Ded/40%	40%/40%+/40%+
Missouri									
Aetna Healthfund CDHP-In-Network		$83.33/$166.66	$1,000/$2,000	$4,000/$8,000	15%	15%	15%	Nothing	$10/$35/$60
Aetna Healthfund CDHP-Out-Network		$83.33/$166.66	$1,000/$2,000	$5,000/$10,000	40%	40%	40%	Fund/Ded/40%	40%/40%+/40%+
Coventry Health Care of Kansas (Kansas City) -HDHP		$83.33/$166.66	$2,500/$5,000	$3,500/$7,000	20%	20%	20%	Nothing	20%/20%/20%
Humana CoverageFirst-In-Network		$83.33	$1,000/$2,000	$3,000/$6,000	$25	$300/day x 5	$150	Nothing	$10/$40/$60
Humana CoverageFirst-Out-Network		N/A	$3,000/$6,000	$4,000/$8,000	30%	30%	30%	30%	$10+/$40+/$60+

High Deductible and Consumer-Driven Health Plans

See pages 74-75 for an explanation of the columns on these pages.

Plan Name	Telephone Number	Enrollment Code		Your Share of Premium			
				Monthly		Biweekly	
		Self only	Self & family	Self only	Self & family	Self only	Self & family
Montana							
Aetna Healthfund CDHP-South/Southeast/Western MT	877-459-6604	H41	H42	157.86	376.78	72.86	173.90
Nebraska							
Aetna Healthfund CDHP-All of Nebraska	877-459-6604	H41	H42	157.86	376.78	72.86	173.90
Nevada							
Aetna Healthfund CDHP-Las Vegas Area	877-459-6604	G51	G52	167.35	398.34	77.24	183.85
New Hampshire							
Aetna Healthfund CDHP-All of New Hampshire	877-459-6604	EP1	EP2	184.12	436.38	84.98	201.41
New Jersey							
Aetna Healthfund CDHP-All of New Jersey	877-459-6604	EP1	EP2	184.12	436.38	84.98	201.41
New Mexico							
Aetna Healthfund CDHP-Albuquerque/Dona Ana/Hobbs Area	877-459-6604	G51	G52	167.35	398.34	77.24	183.85
New York							
Aetna Healthfund CDHP-Most of New York	877-459-6604	EP1	EP2	184.12	436.38	84.98	201.41
Independent Health Assoc -HDHP- Western New York	800-501-3439	QA4	QA5	99.12	258.13	45.75	119.14
North Carolina							
Aetna Healthfund CDHP-All of North Carolina	877-459-6604	F51	F52	158.71	378.69	73.25	174.78

The information contained in this Guide is not the official statement of benefits. Each plan's Federal brochure is the official statement of benefits.

Plan Name	Benefit Type	Premium Contribution to HSA/HRA	CY Ded. Self/Family	Cat. Limit Self/Family	Office Visit	Inpatient Hospital	Outpatient Surgery	Preventive Services	Prescription Drugs Levels I, II, III
Montana									
Aetna Healthfund CDHP-In-Network		$83.33/$166.66	$1,000/$2,000	$4,000/$8,000	15%	15%	15%	Nothing	$10/$35/$60
Aetna Healthfund CDHP-Out-Network		$83.33/$166.66	$1,000/$2,000	$5,000/$10,000	40%	40%	40%	Fund/Ded/40%	40%/40%+/40%+
Nebraska									
Aetna Healthfund CDHP-In-Network		$83.33/$166.66	$1,000/$2,000	$4,000/$8,000	15%	15%	15%	Nothing	$10/$35/$60
Aetna Healthfund CDHP-Out-Network		$83.33/$166.66	$1,000/$2,000	$5,000/$10,000	40%	40%	40%	Fund/Ded/40%	40%/40%+/40%+
Nevada									
Aetna Healthfund CDHP-In-Network		$83.33/$166.66	$1,000/$2,000	$4,000/$8,000	15%	15%	15%	Nothing	$10/$35/$60
Aetna Healthfund CDHP-Out-Network		$83.33/$166.66	$1,000/$2,000	$5,000/$10,000	40%	40%	40%	Fund/Ded/40%	40%/40%+/40%+
New Hampshire									
Aetna Healthfund CDHP-In-Network		$83.33/$166.66	$1,000/$2,000	$4,000/$8,000	15%	15%	15%	Nothing	$10/$35/$60
Aetna Healthfund CDHP-Out-Network		$83.33/$166.66	$1,000/$2,000	$5,000/$10,000	40%	40%	40%	Fund/Ded/40%	40%/40%+/40%+
New Jersey									
Aetna Healthfund CDHP-In-Network		$83.33/$166.66	$1,000/$2,000	$4,000/$8,000	15%	15%	15%	Nothing	$10/$35/$60
Aetna Healthfund CDHP-Out-Network		$83.33/$166.66	$1,000/$2,000	$5,000/$10,000	40%	40%	40%	Fund/Ded/40%	40%/40%+/40%+
New Mexico									
Aetna Healthfund CDHP-In-Network		$83.33/$166.66	$1,000/$2,000	$4,000/$8,000	15%	15%	15%	Nothing	$10/$35/$60
Aetna Healthfund CDHP-Out-Network		$83.33/$166.66	$1,000/$2,000	$5,000/$10,000	40%	40%	40%	Fund/Ded/40%	40%/40%+/40%+
New York									
Aetna Healthfund CDHP-In-Network		$83.33/$166.66	$1,000/$2,000	$4,000/$8,000	15%	15%	15%	Nothing	$10/$35/$60
Aetna Healthfund CDHP-Out-Network		$83.33/$166.66	$1,000/$2,000	$5,000/$10,000	40%	40%	40%	Fund/Ded/40%	40%/40%+/40%+
Independent Health Assoc.-In-Network		$66.42/$166.67	$2,000/$4,000	$5,000/$10,000	$15	Nothing	20%	Nothing	$7/$25/$40
Independent Health Assoc.-Out-Network		$66.42/$166.67	$2,000/$4,000	$5,000/$10,000	40%	40%	40%	Nothing	N/A
North Carolina									
Aetna Healthfund CDHP-In-Network		$83.33/$166.66	$1,000/$2,000	$4,000/$8,000	15%	15%	15%	Nothing	$10/$35/$60
Aetna Healthfund CDHP-Out-Network		$83.33/$166.66	$1,000/$2,000	$5,000/$10,000	40%	40%	40%	Fund/Ded/40%	40%/40%+/40%+

High Deductible and Consumer-Driven Health Plans

See pages 74-75 for an explanation of the columns on these pages.

| Plan Name | Telephone Number | Enrollment Code | | Your Share of Premium | | | |
| | | | | Monthly | | Biweekly | |
		Self only	Self & family	Self only	Self & family	Self only	Self & family
North Dakota							
Aetna Healthfund CDHP-Most of North Dakota	877-459-6604	H41	H42	157.86	376.78	72.86	173.90
Ohio							
AultCare HMO -HDHP- Stark/Carroll/Holmes/Tuscarawas/Wayne Co.	330-363-6360	3A4	3A5	82.25	164.80	37.96	76.06
Oregon							
Aetna Healthfund CDHP-Most of Oregon	877-459-6604	H41	H42	157.86	376.78	72.86	173.90
Pennsylvania							
Aetna Healthfund CDHP-All of Pennsylvania	877-459-6604	H41	H42	157.86	376.78	72.86	173.90
HealthAmerica Pennsylvania-HDHP- Greater Pittsburgh Area	866-351-5946	Y61	Y62	119.14	274.30	54.99	126.60
UPMC Health Plan -HDHP- Western Pennsylvania	877-648-9641	8W4	8W5	123.93	278.97	57.20	128.75
Rhode Island							
Aetna Healthfund CDHP-All of Rhode Island	877-459-6604	EP1	EP2	184.12	436.38	84.98	201.41
South Dakota							
Aetna Healthfund CDHP-Rapid City/Sioux Falls Area	877-459-6604	G51	G52	167.35	398.34	77.24	183.85
Tennessee							
Aetna Healthfund CDHP-Most of Tennessee	877-459-6604	F51	F52	158.71	378.69	73.25	174.78

The information contained in this Guide is not the official statement of benefits. Each plan's Federal brochure is the official statement of benefits.

Plan Name	Benefit Type	Premium Contribution to HSA/HRA	CY Ded. Self/Family	Cat. Limit Self/Family	Office Visit	Inpatient Hospital	Outpatient Surgery	Preventive Services	Prescription Drugs Levels I, II, III
North Dakota									
Aetna Healthfund CDHP-In-Network		$83.33/$166.66	$1,000/$2,000	$4,000/$8,000	15%	15%	15%	Nothing	$10/$35/$60
Aetna Healthfund CDHP-Out-Network		$83.33/$166.66	$1,000/$2,000	$5,000/$10,000	40%	40%	40%	Fund/Ded/40%	40%/40%+/40%+
Ohio									
AultCare HMO-In-Network		$79.08/$158.41	$2,000/$4,000	$4,000/$8,000	20%	20%	20%	Nothing	20%/20%/20%
AultCare HMO-Out-Network		$79.08/$158.41	$4,000/$8,000	$8,000/$16,000	40% UCR	40% UCR	40% UCR	50% UCR	20% Plan Allow
Oregon									
Aetna Healthfund CDHP-In-Network		$83.33/$166.66	$1,000/$2,000	$4,000/$8,000	15%	15%	15%	Nothing	$10/$35/$60
Aetna Healthfund CDHP-Out-Network		$83.33/$166.66	$1,000/$2,000	$5,000/$10,000	40%	40%	40%	Fund/Ded/40%	40%/40%+/40%+
Pennsylvania									
Aetna Healthfund CDHP-In-Network		$83.33/$166.66	$1,000/$2,000	$4,000/$8,000	15%	15%	15%	Nothing	$10/$35/$60
Aetna Healthfund CDHP-Out-Network		$83.33/$166.66	$1,000/$2,000	$5,000/$10,000	40%	40%	40%	Fund/Ded/40%	40%/40%+/40%+
HealthAmerica Pennsylvania-HDHP		$52.09/$104.17	$1,500/$3,000	$4,000/$8,000	$15	None	Nothing	Nothing	$5/$35/$50
UPMC Health Plan-In-Network		$83.33/$166.67	$2,000/$4,000	$3,000/$6,000	10% after Deduct	10% after Ded	100% after Ded	Nothing	$5/$35/$70
UPMC Health Plan-Out-Network		$83.33/$166.67	$2,000/$4,000	$6,000/$12,000	30% after Deduct	30% after Ded	30% after Ded	30%	N/A
Rhode Island									
Aetna Healthfund CDHP-In-Network		$83.33/$166.66	$1,000/$2,000	$4,000/$8,000	15%	15%	15%	Nothing	$10/$35/$60
Aetna Healthfund CDHP-Out-Network		$83.33/$166.66	$1,000/$2,000	$5,000/$10,000	40%	40%	40%	Fund/Ded/40%	40%/40%+/40%+
South Dakota									
Aetna Healthfund CDHP-In-Network		$83.33/$166.66	$1,000/$2,000	$4,000/$8,000	15%	15%	15%	Nothing	$10/$35/$60
Aetna Healthfund CDHP-Out-Network		$83.33/$166.66	$1,000/$2,000	$5,000/$10,000	40%	40%	40%	Fund/Ded/40%	40%/40%+/40%+
Tennessee									
Aetna Healthfund CDHP-In-Network		$83.33/$166.66	$1,000/$2,000	$4,000/$8,000	15%	15%	15%	Nothing	$10/$35/$60
Aetna Healthfund CDHP-Out-Network		$83.33/$166.66	$1,000/$2,000	$5,000/$10,000	40%	40%	40%	Fund/Ded/40%	40%/40%+/40%+

High Deductible and Consumer-Driven Health Plans

See pages 74-75 for an explanation of the columns on these pages.

Plan Name	Telephone Number	Enrollment Code		Your Share of Premium			
				Monthly		Biweekly	
		Self only	Self & family	Self only	Self & family	Self only	Self & family
Texas							
Humana CoverageFirst -CDHP- Corpus Christi Area	888-393-6765	TP1	TP2	122.24	271.97	56.42	125.52
Humana CoverageFirst -CDHP- San Antonio Area	888-393-6765	TU1	TU2	123.15	274.02	56.84	126.47
Humana CoverageFirst -CDHP- Austin Area	888-393-6765	TV1	TV2	129.31	287.72	59.68	132.79
Utah							
Aetna Healthfund CDHP-Most of Utah	877-459-6604	G51	G52	167.35	398.34	77.24	183.85
Altius Health Plans -HDHP- Wasatch Front	800-577-4161	9K4	9K5	87.04	180.33	40.17	83.23
Vermont							
Aetna Healthfund CDHP-All of Vermont	877-459-6604	EP1	EP2	184.12	436.38	84.98	201.41
Virginia							
Aetna Healthfund CDHP-Most of Virginia	877-459-6604	F51	F52	158.71	378.69	73.25	174.78
CareFirst BlueChoice-HDHP-Northern Virginia	888-789-9065	B61	B62	127.44	284.25	58.82	131.19
Washington							
Aetna Healthfund CDHP-Most of Washington	877-459-6604	G51	G52	167.35	398.34	77.24	183.85
KPS Health Plans -HDHP- All of Washington	800-552-7114	L14	L15	100.22	218.99	46.25	101.07

The information contained in this Guide is not the official statement of benefits. Each plan's Federal brochure is the official statement of benefits.

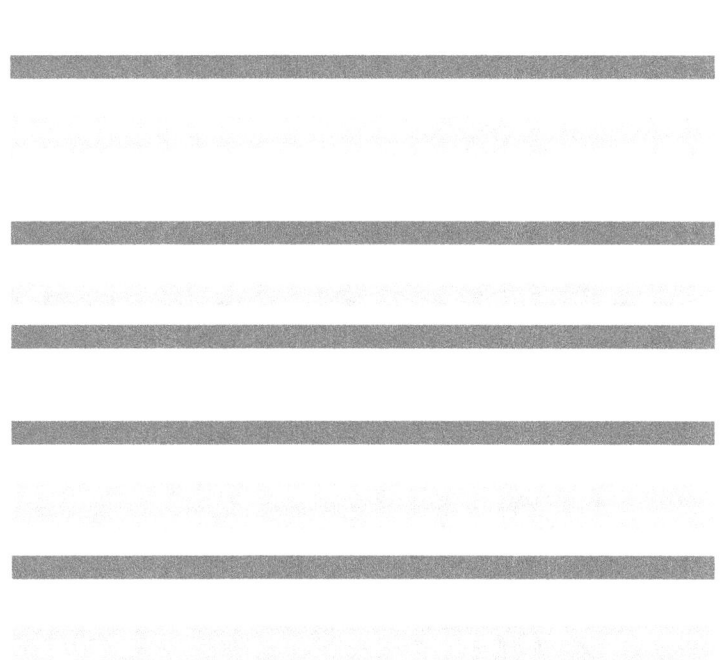

Plan Name	Benefit Type	Premium Contribution to HSA/HRA	CY Ded. Self/Family	Cat. Limit Self/Family	Office Visit	Inpatient Hospital	Outpatient Surgery	Preventive Services	Prescription Drugs Levels I, II, III
Texas									
Humana CoverageFirst-In-Network		$83.33	$1,000/$2,000	$3,000/$6,000	$25	$300/day x 5	$150	Nothing	$10/$40/$60
Humana CoverageFirst-Out-Network		N/A	$3,000/$6,000	$4,000/$8,000	30%	30%	30%	30%	$10+/$40+/$60+
Humana CoverageFirst-In-Network		$83.33	$1,000/$2,000	$3,000/$6,000	$25	$300/day x 5	$150	Nothing	$10/$40/$60
Humana CoverageFirst-Out-Network		N/A	$3,000/$6,000	$4,000/$8,000	30%	30%	30%	30%	$10+/$40+/$60+
Humana CoverageFirst-In-Network		$83.33	$1,000/$2,000	$3,000/$6,000	$25	$300/day x 5	$150	Nothing	$10/$40/$60
Humana CoverageFirst-Out-Network		N/A	$3,000/$6,000	$4,000/$8,000	30%	30%	30%	30%	$10+/$40+/$60+
Utah									
Aetna Healthfund CDHP-In-Network		$83.33/$166.66	$1,000/$2,000	$4,000/$8,000	15%	15%	15%	Nothing	$10/$35/$60
Aetna Healthfund CDHP-Out-Network		$83.33/$166.66	$1,000/$2,000	$5,000/$10,000	40%	40%	40%	Fund/Ded/40%	40%/40%+/40%+
Altius Health Plans		$45.83/$91.66	$1,250/$2,500	$5,000/$10,000	$20	10%	10%	Nothing	$7/$25/$50
Vermont									
Aetna Healthfund CDHP-In-Network		$83.33/$166.66	$1,000/$2,000	$4,000/$8,000	15%	15%	15%	Nothing	$10/$35/$60
Aetna Healthfund CDHP-Out-Network		$83.33/$166.66	$1,000/$2,000	$5,000/$10,000	40%	40%	40%	Fund/Ded/40%	40%/40%+/40%
Virginia									
Aetna Healthfund CDHP-In-Network		$83.33/$166.66	$1,000/$2,000	$4,000/$8,000	15%	15%	15%	Nothing	$10/$35/$60
Aetna Healthfund CDHP-Out-Network		$83.33/$166.66	$1,000/$2,000	$5,000/$10,000	40%	40%	40%	Fund/Ded/40%	40%/40%+/40%+
CareFirst BlueChoice-In-Network		$37.50/$75.00	$1,500/$3,000	$4,000/$8,000	Nothing	$300	Nothing	Nothing	0/$25/$45
CareFirst BlueChoice-Out-Network		$37.50/$75.00	$3,000/$6,000	$6,000/$12,000	$70	$500	$70	Ded, then Nothing	0/$25/$45
Washington									
Aetna Healthfund CDHP-In-Network		$83.33/$166.66	$1,000/$2,000	$4,000/$8,000	15%	15%	15%	Nothing	$10/$35/$60
Aetna Healthfund CDHP-Out-Network		$83.33/$166.66	$1,000/$2,000	$5,000/$10,000	40%	40%	40%	Fund/Ded/40%	40%/40%+/40%+
KPS Health Plans-In-Network		$62.50/$125	$1,500/$3,000	$5,000/$10,000	20%	None	20%	Nothing	$10/$35/50%/$40 max $100
KPS Health Plans-Out-Network		$62.50/$125	$1,500/$3,000	$5,000/$10,000	40%	None	40%	Not Covered	Not Covered

High Deductible and Consumer-Driven Health Plans

See pages 74-75 for an explanation of the columns on these pages.

| | Telephone Number | Enrollment Code | | Your Share of Premium | | | |
| | | | | Monthly | | Biweekly | |
Plan Name		Self only	Self & family	Self only	Self & family	Self only	Self & family
West Virgina							
Aetna Healthfund CDHP-Most of West Virgina	877-459-6604	F51	F52	158.71	378.69	73.25	174.78
Wyoming							
Aetna Healthfund CDHP-All of Wyoming	877-459-6604	H41	H42	157.86	376.78	72.86	173.90
Altius Health Plans -HDHP- Uinta County	800-377-4161	9K4	9K5	87.04	180.33	40.17	83.23

The information contained in this Guide is not the official statement of benefits. Each plan's Federal brochure is the official statement of benefits.

Plan Name	Benefit Type	Premium Contribution to HSA/HRA	CY Ded. Self/Family	Cat. Limit Self/Family	Office Visit	Inpatient Hospital	Outpatient Surgery	Preventive Services	Prescription Drugs Levels I, II, III
West Virgina									
Aetna Healthfund CDHP-In-Network		$83.33/$166.66	$1,000/$2,000	$4,000/$8,000	15%	15%	15%	Nothing	$10/$35/$60
Aetna Healthfund CDHP-Out-Network		$83.33/$166.66	$1,000/$2,000	$5,000/$10,000	40%	40%	40%	Fund/Ded/40%	40%/40%+/40%+
Wyoming									
Aetna Healthfund CDHP-In-Network		$83.33/$166.66	$1,000/$2,000	$4,000/$8,000	15%	15%	15%	Nothing	$10/$35/$60
Aetna Healthfund CDHP-Out-Network		$83.33/$166.66	$1,000/$2,000	$5,000/$10,000	40%	40%	40%	Fund/Ded/40%	40%/40%+/40%+
Altius Health Plans		$45.83/$91.66	$1,250/$2,500	$5,000/$10,000	$20	10%	10%	Nothing	$7/$25/$50

This page intentionally left blank

Appendix F
FEDVIP Program Features

Waiting Periods

Dental - limited only to orthodontic services on most plans; for all other services, you may use your benefits as soon as your coverage becomes effective. There are very few pre-existing condition limitations.

Vision - no waiting period, you may use your benefits as soon as your coverage becomes effective. There are no pre-existing condition limitations.

A Choice of Coverage

Choose between Self Only, Self Plus One or Self and Family.

Contributions

There are no Government contributions. The enrollee pays 100% of the premium.

Salary Deduction

You automatically pay your premium through a payroll deduction using pre-tax dollars; employees cannot elect to waive this pre-tax option and annuitants are not eligible for this option. When premium contributions are withheld on a pre-tax basis, Internal Revenue Service (IRS) guidelines affect your ability to change coverage, i.e., you may cancel or change coverage levels only during a FEDVIP Open Season. You may also make changes throughout the plan year if a qualified life event occurs.

Annual Enrollment Opportunity

Each year, you may enroll or change your dental and/or vision plan enrollment. Open Season runs from the Monday of the second full work week in November through the Monday of the second full work week in December. Other events allow for certain types of changes throughout the year.

Continued Coverage

Eligibility for you or your family member may continue following your retirement or changes in employment status.

Claim Dispute Resolution

The claim review process will differ among plans. Upon written request from the enrollee and as a final option, the carrier will submit a dispute for resolution through a binding arbitration process. OPM will not review nor resolve disputes regarding FEDVIP. Please see your plan brochure for details.

Appendix G
FEDVIP Definitions

Eligible Dependents – Your spouse and unmarried dependent children under age 22. Under certain circumstances, you may also continue coverage for a disabled child 22 years of age or older who is incapable of self-support. **Please Note:** *The health care law does not change the age or unmarried requirement for dependents under FEDVIP.*

First Payer – Under this rule, the FEHB plan is considered the primary payer and pays first, while the FEDVIP plan is considered the secondary payer. No more than 100% of any claim is paid by both plans.

In-Network Services – Services provided by members of the plan's provider network.

Nationwide Plan – A plan which provides services throughout the United States and around the world.

Out-of-Network Services – Services provided by health care professionals who are not a member of the plan's provider network.

Plan – The insurance company which participates in the FEDVIP program. Also called carrier.

Precertification – Also called predetermination. This is the procedure used by dental offices to determine what services a plan will cover and how much will be paid before the service is rendered.

Provider – A licensed health care professional; for example: dentists, oral surgeons, optometrists and ophthalmologists.

Provider Network – A group of health care providers who have a contract with a specific plan to provide services at an agreed upon cost.

Qualifying Life Event (QLE) – An event that allows you to enroll, or if you are already enrolled, allows you to change your enrollment outside of an Open Season. There is no QLE under FEDVIP which allows for cancellation, except upon deployment to active military duty or transitions to certain agencies.

Regional Plan – A plan which provides services only in specified geographic regions.

Usual, Customary and Reasonable – A widely used method, which may vary from company to company, for determining benefit reimbursement levels. The initials simply mean:

Usual. The fee that an individual dentist most frequently charges for a given dental service.

Customary. A fee determined by the insurance company based on the range of usual fees charged by dentists in the same geographic area.

Reasonable. A fee which is justifiable considering special circumstances of the particular care rendered.

Waiting Period – The length of time a person must be covered under the plan before they are eligible for certain benefits. For example, most plans have a 24 month waiting period for orthodontic benefits. This means that you must be covered continuously by the same plan and option for 24 months before your child is eligible for orthodontic coverage.

Appendix H
FEDVIP Qualifying Life Events for Enrollment Changes

A qualifying life event (QLE) is an event that allows you to enroll, or if you are already enrolled, allows you to change your enrollment outside of an Open Season.

The following chart lists the QLEs and the enrollment actions you may take.

Qualifying Life Event	From Not Enrolled to Enrolled	Increase Enrollment Type	Decrease Enrollment Type	Cancel	Change from One Plan to Another
Acquiring an eligible family member	No	Yes	No	No	No
Losing a covered family member	No	No	Yes	No	No
Losing other dental/vision coverage (eligible or covered person)	Yes	Yes	No	No	No
Moving out of regional plan's service area	No	No	No	No	Yes
Going on active military duty, non-pay status (enrollee or spouse)	No	No	No	Yes	No
Returning to pay status from active military duty (enrollee or spouse)	Yes	No	No	No	No
Annuity/ compensation restored	Yes	Yes	Yes	No	No
Transferring to an eligible position	No	No	No	Yes	No

The time frame for requesting a QLE change is from 31 days before to 60 days after the event. There are two exceptions:

- There is no time limit for a change based on moving from a regional plans service area; and
- You cannot request a new enrollment based on a QLE before the QLE occurs except for enrollment due to a loss of dental or vision insurance. You must make the change no later than 60 days after the event.

Generally, enrollments and enrollment changes made based on a QLE are effective on the first day of the pay period following the one in which BENEFEDS receives and confirms the enrollment or change. BENEFEDS will send you confirmation of your new coverage effective date. BENEFEDS is a secure enrollment website sponsored by OPM.

Cancelling an enrollment

You can cancel your enrollment only during the annual Open Season, upon deployment to active military duty, or transfers to certain agencies. An eligible family members coverage also ends upon the effective date of the cancellation.

Appendix I
FEDVIP Plan Comparison Charts

This is a brief summary of the features of the dental and vision plans. Before making a final decision, please read the plan brochures and provider directories thoroughly. All plans are not the same. All benefits are subject to the definitions, limitations, copayments, annual maximums and exclusions set forth in the individual plan brochures. Go to our website at www.opm.gov/insure/dental/rates to find the rating region assigned to the area where you live and the related premium cost you will pay for dental coverage. Go to www.opm.gov/insure/vision/rates to see the premium cost for vision coverage.

Reading the Chart:

The table on the following pages highlights the selected features/classes of dental and/or vision services. Always consult plan brochures before making a decision. The chart does not show all of your possible out-of-pocket costs.

Dental Insurance

The deductibles shown for the dental plans are the amount of covered expenses that you pay before the plan begins to pay. Service Class refers to the level of benefits for each plan. The Service Classes are listed below. Calendar year maximum refers to the annual amount of benefits that you can receive per person.

Please Note: Most plans require that you are continuously enrolled in the same dental plan and/or option for the full waiting period before accessing orthodontia services. There are no other waiting periods for services.

Dental plans provide a comprehensive range of services, including but not limited to the following:

- Class A (Basic) services, which include oral examinations, prophylaxis, diagnostic evaluations, sealants and x-rays.
- Class B (Intermediate) services, which include restorative procedures such as fillings, prefabricated stainless steel crowns, periodontal scaling, tooth extractions, and denture adjustments.
- Class C (Major) services, which include endodontic services such as root canals, periodontal services such as gingivectomy, major restorative services such as crowns, oral surgery, bridges and prosthodontic services such as complete dentures.
- Class D (Orthodontic) services with up to a 24-month waiting period for children up to age 19.

Please review the dental plans' benefits material for detailed information on the benefits covered, cost-sharing requirements and provider directories.

Vision Insurance

Vision plans provide comprehensive eye examinations and coverage for lenses, frames and contact lenses (in lieu of eye glasses). Other benefits, such as discounts on lasik surgery, may also be available.

Please review the vision plans' benefits material for detailed information on the benefits covered, cost-sharing requirements and provider directories.

Appendix I
Federal Employees Dental and Vision Insurance Program (FEDVIP)

Nationwide and International Dental Plans Open to All

Plan Name	Telephone & Website	You pay:					Calendar Year Maximum
		Class A	Class B	Class C	Class D	Deductible	
Aetna High (In-Network Benefits)	1-877-459-6604 www.aetnafeds.com	0%	40%	60%	70%	$0	$3,000 per year per person - in-network $2,000 per year per person - out-of-network $1,500 lifetime max per person (orthodontic services only) 24-month waiting period for orthodontia services
Aetna High (Out-of-Network Benefits)		0%	40%	60%	70%	$0	
GEHA Standard (In-Network Benefits)	1-877-434-2336 www.gehadental.com	0%	45%	65%	30%	$0	$12,000 per year per person (high option) or $2,500 per year per person (standard option) $2,500 lifetime max per person (high option orthodontic services only)
GEHA Standard (Out-of-Network Benefits)		0%	45%	65%	30%	$0	$1,500 lifetime max per person (standard option orthodontic services only) 12 month waiting period for orthodontia services
GEHA High (In-Network Benefits)		0%	20%	50%	30%	$0	
GEHA High (Out-of-Network Benefits)		0%	20%	50%	30%	$0	
MetLife Standard (In-Network Benefits)	1-888-865-6854 www.federaldental.metlife.com	0%	45%	65%	50%	$0	$1,200 standard option in-network annual non-orthodontic maximum per person $1,500 standard option in-network lifetime max per person for orthodontics $600 standard option out-network annual non-orthodontic maximum
MetLife Standard (Out-of-Network Benefits)		40%	60%	80%	50%	$100/person	per person $1,000 standard option out-of-network lifetime max per person for orthodontics $10,000 high option in-network annual non-orthodontic maximum
MetLife High (In-Network Benefits)		0%	30%	50%	50%	$0	per person $3,500 high option in-network lifetime max per person for orthodontics $10,000 high option out-of-network annual non-orthodontic maximum per person
MetLife High (Out-of-Network Benefits)		10%	40%	60%	50%	$50/person	$3,500 high option out-of-network lifetime max per person for orthodontics There is no calendar year deductible for Class D services 24-month waiting period for orthodontia services
United Concordia High (In-Network Benefits)	1-877-438-8224 (Open Season) 1-877-394-8224 (General) www.uccifedvip.com	0%	20%	50%	50%	$0	$3,500 per year per person $1,500 lifetime max per person (orthodontic services only) 24-month waiting period for orthodontia services
United Concordia High (Out-of-Network Benefits)		20%	40%	60%	50%	$0	

Please Note: Out-of-Network Benefits — members are responsible for paying the difference between the plan's payment and the non-network provider's billed charges.

Appendix I
Federal Employees Dental and Vision Insurance Program (FEDVIP)

Regional Dental Plans *Only Open to Persons Living in Specific Geographic Areas*

Plan Name	Telephone & Website	Class A	Class B	Class C	Class D	Deductible	Calendar Year Maximum
Humana High (Open to residents of the Southeastern, Midwestern, and Mid-Atlantic states)	1-877-692-2468 www.feds.humana.com	0%	Flat Rate Approx 25%	Flat Rate Approx 35%	Flat Rate Approx 50%	$0	$15,000 per year per person Unlimited lifetime orthodontic coverage Out-of-network benefits NOT provided No waiting period for orthodontia services
GHI High (In-network benefits) (Open to NY and Northern NJ residents and parts of CT and PA)	212-501-4444 www.ghi.com	0%	0%	0%	0%	$0	$2,500 per year per person $2,000 lifetime max per person (orthodontic services only) Out-of-network benefits available – paid at the same in-network rate 12-month waiting period for orthodontia services
GHI High (Out-of-network benefits)		0%	0%	0%	0%	$50 self/$150 self & family/self plus one Class B and Class C	
Triple-S Salud High (Open to Puerto Rico residents)	787-774-6060 787-749-4777 1-800-981-3241 TTY 787-792-1370 TTY 1-866-215-1999 www.ssspr.com	0%	30%	60% / 30%	50%	$0	No maximum $2,000 lifetime max per person (orthodontic services only) Out-of-network benefits NOT provided 24 month waiting period for orthodontia services

Please Note: Out-of-Network Benefits – members are responsible for paying the difference between the plan's payment and the non-network provider's billed charges.

Appendix I
Federal Employees Dental and Vision Insurance Program (FEDVIP)

Nationwide and International Vision Plans Open to All

The table below highlights the selected features of available vision plans. Always consult plan brochures before making a decision. The chart does not show all of your possible out-of-pocket costs.

Vision plans provide comprehensive eye examinations and coverage for lenses, frames and contact lenses (in lieu of eye glasses). There are no deductibles or waiting periods. Other benefits such as discounts on lasik surgery may also be available.

Plan Name	Frames	Lenses	Exams	Co-payments	Covered Lens Options	Additional Features
FEP BlueVision Standard	Every 24 months	Every 12 months	Every 12 months	$0	Single Lined Bifocal Lined Trifocal Lenticular UV Coating Scratch-resistant coating	Breakage warranty; Laser vision correction discount; low vision coverage. $130 plus 20% of remaining cost frame allowance Additional lens options covered with a co-pay. Out-of-network benefits NOT provided Flat rate reimbursement in limited access areas and internationally FSAFEDS paperless reimbursement available
FEP BlueVision High	Every 12 months	Every 12 months	Every 12 months	$0	Single Lined Bifocal Lined Trifocal Lenticular Standard Progressives UV Coating Scratch-resistant coating Transitions®	Breakage warranty; Laser vision correction discount; low vision coverage. $150 plus 20% of remaining cost frame allowance $150 allowance to purchase contact lenses (materials) Additional lens options covered with a co-pay. Out-of-network benefits available at a lower rate Flat rate reimbursement in limited access areas and internationally FSAFEDS paperless reimbursement available
UnitedHealthcare Vision Plan Standard	Every 12 months	Every 12 months	Every 12 months	$10 exam/ $25 material	Single Lined Bifocal Lined Trifocal Lenticular Polycarbonate Scratch-resistant Coating Lenses that transition to light	Low vision; prosthetic eye; vision therapy; Laser vision correction discount. $130 frame allowance Additional lens option discounts Out-of-network benefits available– paid at a lower rate Flat rate reimbursement for international, out-of-network and limited access services
UnitedHealthcare Vision Plan High	Every 12 months	Every 12 months	Every 12 months	$10 exam/ $10 material	Single Lined Bifocal Lined Trifocal Lenticular Polycarbonate Scratch-resistant Coating Tinted Lenses UV Coating Lenses that transition to light	Low vision; prosthetic eye; vision therapy; Laser vision correction discount. $130 frame allowance Additional lens option discounts Out-of-network benefits available– paid at a lower rate Flat rate reimbursement for international, out-of-network and limited access services
VSP (Vision Service Plan) Standard	Every 12 months	Every 12 months	Every 12 months	$10 exam/ $20 material	Single Lined Bifocal Lined Trifocal Lenticular Polycarbonate Scratch-resistant Coating	Laser vision correction discount. $120 frame allowance $120 allowance for contacts and contact lens exam Additional lenses options covered at a discount. Out-of-network benefits available – paid at a lower rate Additional lens option and contact lens exam discounts Additional prescription glasses and sunglasses discounts FSAFEDS paperless reimbursement available
VSP (Vision Service Plan) High	Every 12 months	Every 12 months	Every 12 months	$10 (including exam and glasses)	Single Lined Bifocal Lined Trifocal Lenticular Polycarbonate Scratch-resistant Coating Anti-reflective Coating Lenses that transition to light UV Coating Select tints	Laser vision correction discount. $150 frame allowance $150 allowance for contacts and contact lens exam Out-of-network benefits available – paid at a lower rate Additional lens option and contact lens exam discounts Additional prescription glasses and sunglasses discounts FSAFEDS paperless reimbursement available

Appendix J
Federal Employees Dental and Vision Insurance Program (FEDVIP) Dental Rating Regional Chart

Rating Areas

State	State/ZIP (first 3)	Aetna	GEHA Std	GEHA High	MetLife Std	MetLife High	United Concordia	Humana	GHI	Triple-S Salud
AK	entire state	5	5	5	5	5	5	#N/A	#N/A	#N/A
AL	356-358	1	1	1	1	1	1	1	#N/A	#N/A
AL	rest of state	2	1	1	1	1	1	1	#N/A	#N/A
AR	entire state	2	1	1	1	1	1	5	#N/A	#N/A
AZ	entire state	3	3	3	1	1	1	2	#N/A	#N/A
CA	900-918, 922-935	3	4	4	5	5	3	4	#N/A	#N/A
CA	919-921	3	4	4	4	4	4	4	#N/A	#N/A
CA	939-941, 943-954	4	5	5	5	5	5	4	#N/A	#N/A
CA	942, 956-958	4	4	4	4	4	4	4	#N/A	#N/A
CA	rest of state	4	4	4	5	5	4	4	#N/A	#N/A
CO	entire state	3	4	4	4	4	3	4	#N/A	#N/A
CT	060-063	5	4	4	5	5	5	#N/A	#N/A	#N/A
CT	064-069	3	5	5	5	5	5	#N/A	1	#N/A
DC	entire state	2	4	4	4	4	4	2	#N/A	#N/A
DE	entire state	2	3	3	3	3	2	#N/A	#N/A	#N/A
FL	327-328, 347	2	2	2	1	1	1	2	#N/A	#N/A
FL	330-334	2	4	4	3	3	3	2	#N/A	#N/A
FL	rest of state	3	2	2	1	1	1	2	#N/A	#N/A
GA	300-303, 311	3	3	3	2	2	1	3	#N/A	#N/A
GA	rest of state	4	2	2	1	1	1	5	#N/A	#N/A
GU	entire state	5	1	1	5	5	5	#N/A	#N/A	#N/A
HI	entire state	4	3	3	4	4	5	#N/A	#N/A	#N/A
IA	entire state	3	1	1	1	1	2	#N/A	#N/A	#N/A
ID	entire state	4	2	2	1	1	2	#N/A	#N/A	#N/A
IL	600-608	2	3	3	4	4	3	1	#N/A	#N/A
IL	620-622	2	2	2	1	1	1	1	#N/A	#N/A
IL	rest of state	3	1	1	1	1	1	1	#N/A	#N/A
IN	460-462	2	2	2	1	1	1	1	#N/A	#N/A
IN	463-464	2	3	3	4	4	3	1	#N/A	#N/A
IN	rest of state	3	1	1	1	1	2	1	#N/A	#N/A
KS	660-662	1	2	2	1	1	2	1	#N/A	#N/A
KS	rest of state	3	1	1	1	1	2	1	#N/A	#N/A
KY	410	2	2	2	1	1	1	1	#N/A	#N/A
KY	rest of state	1	1	1	1	1	1	1	#N/A	#N/A

Appendix J
Federal Employees Dental and Vision Insurance Program (FEDVIP)
Dental Rating Regional Chart

Rating Areas

State	State/ZIP (first 3)	Aetna	GEHA Std	GEHA High	MetLife Std	MetLife High	United Concordia	Humana	GHI	Triple-S Salud
LA	entire state	2	2	2	1	1	1	5	#N/A	#N/A
MA	entire state	5	4	4	5	5	5	#N/A	#N/A	#N/A
MD	206-218	2	4	4	4	4	4	2	#N/A	#N/A
MD	219	2	3	3	3	3	2	#N/A	#N/A	#N/A
MD	rest of state	2	2	2	2	2	4	#N/A	#N/A	#N/A
ME	entire state	5	3	3	2	2	3	#N/A	#N/A	#N/A
MI	480-485	3	3	3	3	3	2	#N/A	#N/A	#N/A
MI	rest of state	3	2	2	2	2	3	#N/A	#N/A	#N/A
MN	550-555	2	3	3	4	4	3	#N/A	#N/A	#N/A
MN	rest of state	3	2	2	2	2	2	#N/A	#N/A	#N/A
MO	630-633	2	2	2	1	1	1	1	#N/A	#N/A
MO	640-641	1	2	2	1	1	2	1	#N/A	#N/A
MO	rest of state	3	1	1	1	1	1	1	#N/A	#N/A
MS	entire state	2	1	1	1	1	1	5	#N/A	#N/A
MT	entire state	4	2	2	1	1	1	#N/A	#N/A	#N/A
NC	entire state	4	2	2	1	1	1	5	#N/A	#N/A
ND	entire state	3	1	1	1	1	2	#N/A	#N/A	#N/A
NE	entire state	1	1	1	1	1	2	#N/A	#N/A	#N/A
NH	entire state	5	4	4	5	5	5	#N/A	#N/A	#N/A
NJ	080-084	2	3	3	3	3	2	#N/A	#N/A	#N/A
NJ	rest of state	3	5	5	5	5	5	#N/A	1	#N/A
NM	entire state	3	3	3	1	1	1	#N/A	#N/A	#N/A
NV	897	4	4	4	4	4	4	#N/A	#N/A	#N/A
NV	rest of state	2	3	3	2	2	2	#N/A	#N/A	#N/A
NY	004, 005	3	5	5	5	5	5	#N/A	1	#N/A
NY	100-119, 124-126	3	5	5	5	5	5	#N/A	1	#N/A
NY	rest of state	4	2	2	2	2	3	#N/A	1	#N/A
OH	430-432	2	2	2	1	1	2	3	#N/A	#N/A
OH	440-443	2	2	2	1	1	3	1	#N/A	#N/A
OH	450-452	2	2	2	1	1	1	1	#N/A	#N/A
OH	453-455	2	2	2	1	1	2	1	#N/A	#N/A
OH	rest of state	3	1	1	1	1	1	1	#N/A	#N/A
OK	entire state	2	2	2	1	1	1	3	#N/A	#N/A
OR	970-973	4	3	3	4	4	5	#N/A	#N/A	#N/A
OR	rest of state	5	3	3	3	3	4	#N/A	#N/A	#N/A

Appendix J
Federal Employees Dental and Vision Insurance Program (FEDVIP)
Dental Rating Regional Chart

Rating Areas

State	State/ZIP (first 3)	Aetna	GEHA Std	GEHA High	MetLife Std	MetLife High	United Concordia	Humana	GHI	Triple-S Salud
PA	150-154, 156, 160	1	1	1	1	1	1	#N/A	#N/A	#N/A
PA	183	3	5	5	5	5	5	#N/A	1	#N/A
PA	189-194	2	3	3	3	3	2	#N/A	#N/A	#N/A
PA	rest of state	3	1	1	1	1	1	#N/A	#N/A	#N/A
PR	entire state	3	1	1	1	1	1	#N/A	#N/A	1
RI	entire state	5	4	4	5	5	5	#N/A	#N/A	#N/A
SC	entire state	4	2	2	1	1	1	5	#N/A	#N/A
SD	entire state	3	1	1	1	1	2	#N/A	#N/A	#N/A
TN	entire state	1	2	2	1	1	1	1	#N/A	#N/A
TX	750-753, 760-762	2	3	3	1	1	1	3	#N/A	#N/A
TX	770-775	2	3	3	1	1	1	3	#N/A	#N/A
TX	rest of state	2	2	2	1	1	1	3	#N/A	#N/A
UT	entire state	2	1	1	1	1	2	1	#N/A	#N/A
VA	201, 220-226	2	4	4	4	4	4	2	#N/A	#N/A
VA	230-232, 238	3	2	2	1	1	2	5	#N/A	#N/A
VA	rest of state	3	2	2	1	1	1	4	#N/A	#N/A
VI	entire state	overseas	1	1	5	5	5	#N/A	#N/A	#N/A
VT	entire state	5	2	2	2	2	3	#N/A	#N/A	#N/A
WA	980-985	5	5	5	5	5	5	#N/A	#N/A	#N/A
WA	986	4	3	3	4	4	5	#N/A	#N/A	#N/A
WA	rest of state	5	4	4	4	4	4	#N/A	#N/A	#N/A
WI	530-534	3	2	2	2	2	3	#N/A	#N/A	#N/A
WI	540	2	3	3	4	4	3	#N/A	#N/A	#N/A
WI	rest of state	3	2	2	2	2	2	#N/A	#N/A	#N/A
WV	entire state	4	2	2	1	1	1	3	#N/A	#N/A
WY	entire state	4	1	1	1	1	2	#N/A	#N/A	#N/A

Appendix K
Federal Employees Dental and Vision Insurance Program (FEDVIP) Premium Rate Charts

Nationwide Dental Rates

Please note: Rating areas for each carrier are not the same for all plans. Please refer to Appendix J to determine your specific region.

Plan Name	Option	Rating Region	Biweekly Premium			Monthly Premium		
			Self Only	Self Plus One	Self & Family	Self Only	Self Plus One	Self & Family
Aetna PPO	High (In and Out-of-Network benefits)	1	$12.48	$24.95	$37.43	$27.04	$54.06	$81.10
		2	$13.74	$27.48	$41.22	$29.77	$59.54	$89.31
		3	$14.63	$29.25	$43.87	$31.70	$63.38	$95.05
		4	$16.14	$32.27	$48.41	$34.97	$69.92	$104.89
		5	$17.52	$35.05	$52.57	$37.96	$75.94	$113.90
GEHA PPO	Standard (In and Out-of-Network benefits)	1	$9.00	$18.00	$27.02	$19.50	$39.00	$58.54
		2	$9.89	$19.78	$29.67	$21.43	$42.86	$64.29
		3	$11.24	$22.46	$33.69	$24.35	$48.66	$73.00
		4	$12.13	$24.25	$36.38	$26.28	$52.54	$78.82
		5	$13.47	$26.94	$40.40	$29.19	$58.37	$87.53
GEHA PPO	High (In and Out-of-Network benefits)	1	$15.25	$30.50	$45.76	$33.04	$66.08	$99.15
		2	$16.77	$33.54	$50.35	$36.34	$72.67	$109.09
		3	$19.04	$38.09	$57.13	$41.25	$82.53	$123.78
		4	$20.56	$41.12	$61.71	$44.55	$89.09	$133.71
		5	$22.84	$45.69	$68.56	$49.49	$99.00	$148.55
MetLife PPO	Standard (In and Out-of-Network benefits)	1	$8.57	$17.17	$25.76	$18.57	$37.20	$55.81
		2	$9.28	$18.57	$27.86	$20.11	$40.24	$60.36
		3	$10.30	$20.56	$30.86	$22.32	$44.55	$66.86
		4	$11.44	$22.87	$34.30	$24.79	$49.55	$74.32
		5	$12.56	$25.12	$37.70	$27.21	$54.43	$81.68
MetLife PPO	High (In and Out-of-Network benefits)	1	$15.82	$31.63	$47.41	$34.28	$68.53	$102.72
		2	$17.70	$35.43	$53.12	$38.35	$76.77	$115.09
		3	$19.30	$38.56	$57.85	$41.82	$83.55	$125.34
		4	$20.89	$41.74	$62.61	$45.26	$90.44	$135.66
		5	$23.39	$46.78	$70.16	$50.68	$101.36	$152.01
United Concordia PPO	High (In and Out-of-Network benefits)	1	$14.10	$28.17	$42.27	$30.55	$61.04	$91.59
		2	$16.19	$32.34	$48.53	$35.08	$70.07	$105.15
		3	$17.59	$35.13	$52.71	$38.11	$76.12	$114.21
		4	$18.98	$37.90	$56.89	$41.12	$82.12	$123.26
		5	$20.46	$40.91	$61.36	$44.33	$88.64	$132.95

Appendix K
Federal Employees Dental and Vision Insurance Program (FEDVIP)
Premium Rate Charts

Regional Dental Rates

Please note: Rating areas for each carrier are not the same for all plans. Please refer to Appendix J to determine your specific region.

Plan Name	Option	Rating Region	Biweekly Premium			Monthly Premium		
			Self Only	Self Plus One	Self & Family	Self Only	Self Plus One	Self & Family
Humana	High (In-Network Benefits only except for emergency services)	1	$9.57	$19.12	$28.69	$20.74	$41.43	$62.16
		2	$10.30	$20.59	$30.89	$22.32	$44.61	$66.93
		3	$10.37	$20.73	$31.10	$22.47	$44.92	$67.38
		4	$14.18	$28.36	$42.54	$30.72	$61.45	$92.17
		5	$14.25	$28.49	$42.74	$30.88	$61.73	$92.60
GHI PPO	High (In-and Out-of-Network Benefits)	1	$17.68	$35.32	$53.00	$38.31	$76.53	$114.83
Triple-S Salud PPO	High (In-Network Benefits only except for services rendered by orthodontists)	1	$4.27	$8.53	$11.17	$9.25	$18.48	$24.20

International Dental Rates

Please note: International premium rates are not regionally based.

Plan Name	Biweekly Premium			Monthly Premium		
	Self Only	Self Plus One	Self & Family	Self Only	Self Plus One	Self & Family
Aetna	$18.74	$37.46	$56.20	$40.60	$81.16	$121.77
GEHA Standard	$9.00	$18.00	$27.02	$19.50	$39.00	$58.54
GEHA High	$15.25	$30.50	$45.76	$33.04	$66.08	$99.15
MetLife Standard	$12.56	$25.12	$37.70	$27.21	$54.43	$81.68
MetLife High	$23.39	$46.78	$70.16	$50.68	$101.36	$152.01
United Concordia	$20.46	$40.91	$61.36	$44.33	$88.64	$132.95

Appendix K
Federal Employees Dental and Vision Insurance Program (FEDVIP)
Premium Rate Charts

Nationwide Vision Rates

Plan Name	Telephone & Website	Plan Option	Biweekly Premium			Monthly Premium		
			Self Only	Self Plus One	Self & Family	Self Only	Self Plus One	Self & Family
FEP BlueVision	1-888-550-2583 www.fepblue.org	Standard High	$3.69 $4.67	$7.36 $9.33	$11.05 $14.01	$8.00 $10.12	$15.95 $20.22	$23.94 $30.36
UnitedHealthcare Vision Plan	1-866-249-1999 TTY: 800-524-3157 www.myuhcvision.com/fedvip	Standard High	$2.92 $4.15	$5.69 $8.08	$8.47 $12.04	$6.33 $8.99	$12.34 $17.51	$18.35 $26.08
VSP (Vision Service Plan)	1-800-807-0764 www.choosevsp.com	Standard High	$3.67 $6.38	$7.31 $12.76	$10.98 $19.14	$7.94 $13.83	$15.84 $27.64	$23.78 $41.47

International Vision Rates

Plan Name	Telephone & Website	Plan Option	Biweekly Premium			Monthly Premium		
			Self Only	Self Plus One	Self & Family	Self Only	Self Plus One	Self & Family
FEP BlueVision	1-888-550-2583 www.fepblue.org	Standard High	$3.69 $4.67	$7.36 $9.33	$11.05 $14.01	$8.00 $10.12	$15.95 $20.22	$23.94 $30.36
UnitedHealthcare Vision Plan	1-866-249-1999 TTY: 800-524-3157 www.myuhcvision.com/fedvip	Standard High	$2.92 $4.15	$5.69 $8.08	$8.47 $12.04	$6.33 $8.99	$12.34 $17.51	$18.35 $26.08
VSP (Vision Service Plan)	1-800-807-0764 www.choosevsp.com	Standard High	$3.67 $6.38	$7.31 $12.76	$10.98 $19.14	$7.94 $13.83	$15.84 $27.64	$23.78 $41.47

Medicaid and the Children's Health Insurance Program (CHIP) Offer Free or Low-Cost Health Coverage to Children and Families

- If you are eligible for health coverage from your employer, but are unable to afford the premiums, some States have premium assistance programs that can help pay for coverage. These States use funds from their Medicaid or CHIP programs to help people who are eligible for employer-sponsored health coverage, but need assistance in paying their health premiums.
- If you or your dependents are already enrolled in Medicaid or CHIP and you live in a State listed below, you can contact your State Medicaid or CHIP office to find out if premium assistance is available.
- If you or your dependents are NOT currently enrolled in Medicaid or CHIP, and you think you or any of your dependents might be eligible for either of these programs, you can contact your State Medicaid or CHIP office or dial **1-877-KIDS NOW** or www.insurekidsnow.gov to find out how to apply. If you qualify, you can ask the State if it has a program that might help you pay the premiums for an employer-sponsored plan.
- Once it is determined that you or your dependents are eligible for premium assistance under Medicaid or CHIP, your employer's health plan is required to permit you and your dependents to enroll in the plan – as long as you and your dependents are eligible, but not already enrolled in the employer's plan. This is called a "special enrollment" opportunity, and **you must request coverage within 60 days of being determined eligible for premium assistance.**

If you live in one of the following States, you may be eligible for assistance paying your employer health plan premiums. The following list of States is current as of January 31, 2013. You should contact your State for further information –

ALABAMA – Medicaid
Website: http://www.medicaid.alabama.gov
Phone: 1-855-692-5447

ALASKA – Medicaid
Website: http://health.hss.state.ak.us/dpa/programs/medicaid/
Phone (Outside of Anchorage): 1-888-318-8890
Phone (Anchorage): 907-269-6529

ARIZONA – CHIP
Website: http://www.azahcccs.gov/applicants
Phone (Outside of Maricopa County): 1-877-764-5437
Phone (Maricopa County): 602-417-5437

COLORADO – Medicaid
Medicaid Website: http://www.colorado.gov/
Medicaid Phone (In state): 1-800-866-3513
Medicaid Phone (Out of state): 1-800-221-3943

FLORIDA – Medicaid
Website: https://www.flmedicaidtplrecovery.com/
Phone: 1-877-357-3268

GEORGIA – Medicaid
Website: http://dch.georgia.gov/
Click on Programs, then Medicaid
Phone: 1-800-869-1150

IDAHO – Medicaid and CHIP
Medicaid Website: www.accesstohealthinsurance.idaho.gov
Medicaid Phone: 1-800-926-2588
CHIP Website: www.medicaid idaho.gov
CHIP Phone: 1-800-926-2588

INDIANA – Medicaid
Website: http://www.in.gov/fssa
Phone: 1-800-889-9948

IOWA – Medicaid
Website: www.dhs.state ia.us/hipp/
Phone: 1-888-346-9562

KANSAS – Medicaid
Website: http://www.kdheks.gov/hcf/
Phone: 1-800-792-4884

KENTUCKY – Medicaid
Website: http://chfs.ky.gov/dms/default.htm
Phone: 1-800-635-2570

LOUISIANA – Medicaid
Website: http://www.lahipp.dhh louisiana.gov
Phone: 1-888-695-2447

MAINE – Medicaid
Website: http://www.maine.gov/dhhs/OIAS/public-assistance/index.html
Phone: 1-800-572-3839

MASSACHUSETTS – Medicaid and CHIP
Website: http://www.mass.gov/MassHealth
Phone: 1-800-462-1120

MINNESOTA – Medicaid
Website: http://www.dhs.state.mn.us/
Click on Health Care, then Medical Assistance
Phone: 1-800-657-3629

MISSOURI – Medicaid
Website: http://www.dss.mo.gov/mhd/participants/pages/hipp.htm
Phone: 573-751-2005

MONTANA – Medicaid
Website: http://medicaidprovider.hhs.mt.gov/clientpages/clientindex.shtml
Phone: 1-800-694-3084

NEBRASKA – Medicaid
Website: http://dhhs.ne.gov/medicaid/Pages/med_kidsconx.aspx
Phone: 1-877-255-3092

NEVADA – Medicaid
Medicaid Website: http://dwss.nv.gov/
Medicaid Phone: 1-800-992-0900

NEW HAMPSHIRE – Medicaid
Website: www.dhhs.nh.gov/ombp/index.htm
Phone: 603-271-5218

Medicaid and the Children's Health Insurance Program (CHIP) Offer Free or Low-Cost Health Coverage to Children and Families

NEW JERSEY – Medicaid and CHIP
Medicaid Website: http://www.state.nj.us/humanservices/dmahs/clients/medicaid/
Medicaid Phone: 1-800-356-1561
CHIP Website: http://www.njfamilycare.org/index.html
CHIP Phone: 1-800-701-0710

NEW YORK – Medicaid
Website: http://www.nyhealth.gov/health_care/medicaid/
Phone: 1-800-541-2831

NORTH CAROLINA – Medicaid and CHIP
Website: http://www.ncdhhs.gov/dma
Phone: 919-855-4100

NORTH DAKOTA – Medicaid
Website: http://www.nd.gov/dhs/services/medicalserv/medicaid/
Phone: 1-800-755-2604

OKLAHOMA – Medicaid and CHIP
Website: http://www.insureoklahoma.org
Phone: 1-888-365-3742

OREGON – Medicaid and CHIP
Website: http://www.oregonhealthykids.gov
http://www.hijossaludablesoregon.gov
Phone: 1-877-314-5678

PENNSYLVANIA – Medicaid
Website: http://www.dpw.state.pa.us/hipp
Phone: 1-800-692-7462

RHODE ISLAND – Medicaid
Website: www.ohhs.ri.gov
Phone: 401-462-5300

SOUTH CAROLINA – Medicaid
Website: http://www.scdhhs.gov
Phone: 1-888-549-0820

SOUTH DAKOTA – Medicaid
Website: http://dss.sd.gov
Phone: 1-888-828-0059

TEXAS – Medicaid
Website: https://www.gethipptexas.com/
Phone: 1-800-440-0493

UTAH – Medicaid and CHIP
Website: http://health.utah.gov/upp
Phone: 1-866-435-7414

VERMONT– Medicaid
Website: http://www.greenmountaincare.org/
Phone: 1-800-250-8427

VIRGINIA – Medicaid and CHIP
Medicaid Website: http://www.dmas.virginia.gov/rcp-HIPP.htm
Medicaid Phone: 1-800-432-5924
CHIP Website: http://www.famis.org/
CHIP Phone: 1-866-873-2647

WASHINGTON – Medicaid
Website: http://hrsa.dshs.wa.gov/premiumpymt/Apply.shtm
Phone: 1-800-562-3022 ext. 15473

WEST VIRGINIA – Medicaid
Website: www.dhhr.wv.gov/bms/
Phone: 1-877-598-5820, HMS Third Party Liability

WISCONSIN – Medicaid
Website: http://www.badgercareplus.org/pubs/p-10095.htm
Phone: 1-800-362-3002

WYOMING – Medicaid
Website: http://health.wyo.gov/healthcarefin/equalitycare
Phone: 307-777-7531

To see if any more States have added a premium assistance program since January 31, 2012, or for more information on special enrollment rights, you can contact either:

U.S. Department of Labor
Employee Benefits Security Administration
www.dol.gov/ebsa
1-866-444-EBSA (3272)

U.S. Department of Health and Human Services
Centers for Medicare & Medicaid Services
www.cms.hhs.gov
1-877-267-2323, Ext. 61565

OMB Control Number 1210-0137 (expires 09/30/2013)

Summary Information

	New Hires Can Enroll	Federal Benefits Open Season	How to Enroll	OPM's Program Website
FEHB	Within 60 days from new hire date	Annual – November 12 to December 10, 2012	Varies by agency; automated enrollment or via SF 2809	**www.opm.gov/insure/health**
FEDVIP	Within 60 days from new hire date	Annual – November 12 to December 10, 2012	Go to www.BENEFEDS.com or call 1-877-888-3337	**www.opm.gov/insure/dental www.opm.gov/insure/vision**
FSAFEDS	Within 60 days from new hire date	Annual – November 12 to December 10, 2012	Go to www.FSAFEDS.com or call 1-877-372-3337	**www.opm.gov/insure/flexible**
FEGLI	Within 60 days from new hire date for optional insurance; automatically enrolled in Basic insurance until you take action to cancel	No annual Open Season	Varies by agency; automated enrollment or via SF 2817 for new hires Others provide medical information on SF 2822	**www.opm.gov/insure/life**
FLTCIP	Apply (not necessarily enroll) within 60 days from new hire date with abbreviated underwriting	No annual Open Season	Go to www.LTCFEDS.com or call 1-800-582-3337	**www.opm.gov/insure/ltc**